Diabetic Meal Prep for Beginners

Simple and Healthy Recipes for Smart People on Diabetic Diet | 30-Day Meal Plan to Prevent and Reverse Diabetes

Adamer Highon

© Copyright 2019 Adamer Highon - All Rights Reserved.

In no way is it legal to reproduce, duplicate, or transmit any part of this document by either electronic means or in printed format. Recording of this publication is strictly prohibited, and any storage of this material is not allowed unless with written permission from the publisher. All rights reserved.

The information provided herein is stated to be truthful and consistent, in that any liability, regarding inattention or otherwise, by any usage or abuse of any policies, processes, or directions contained within is the solitary and complete responsibility of the recipient reader. Under no circumstances will any legal liability or blame be held against the publisher for any reparation, damages, or monetary loss due to the information herein, either directly or indirectly.

Respective authors own all copyrights not held by the publisher.

Legal Notice:

This book is copyright protected. This is only for personal use. You cannot amend, distribute, sell, use, quote or paraphrase any part of the content within this book without the consent of the author or copyright owner. Legal action will be pursued if this is breached.

Disclaimer Notice:

Please note the information contained within this document is for educational and entertainment purposes only. Every attempt has been made to provide accurate, up-to-date and reliable, complete information. No warranties of any kind are expressed or implied. Readers acknowledge that the author is not engaging in the rendering of legal, financial, medical or professional advice.

By reading this document, the reader agrees that under no circumstances are we responsible for any losses, direct or indirect, which are incurred as a result of the use of information contained within this document, including, but not limited to, errors, omissions, or inaccuracies.

Table of contents

Introduction 8
Chapter 1: Understanding Diabetes 10
    What is Diabetes? 10
    Types of Diabetes 10
    How to Identify if you have Diabetes 12
    Risk Factors 13
    The Link between Obesity and Type 2 Diabetes 15
    How can Diabetes be Prevented and Controlled 15
    A Healthy Meal Can Help Ease the Effects of Diabetes 17
    Food to Eat 18
    Food to Avoid 18
Chapter 2: Why Meal Prep? 20
Chapter 3: The Common Mistakes by Meal Prepping Beginners 22
Chapter 4: The Benefits of the Diabetes Meal Prep 24
Chapter 5: 30-Day Meal Plan 26
Chapter 6: Breakfast 32
    Granola with Fruits 32
    Apple & Cinnamon Pancake 33
    Spinach Scramble 34
    Breakfast Parfait 35
    Asparagus & Cheese Omelet 36
    Sausage, Egg & Potatoes 37
    Cucumber & Yogurt 38
    Yogurt Breakfast Pudding 39
    Vegetable Omelet 40

Almond & Berry Smoothie 41

Chapter 7: Meat Recipes 42

Pork Chops with Grape Sauce 42

Roasted Pork & Apples 44

Pork with Cranberry Relish 45

Irish Pork Roast 46

Sesame Pork with Mustard Sauce 47

Steak with Mushroom Sauce 48

Steak with Tomato & Herbs 49

Barbecue Beef Brisket 50

Beef & Asparagus 51

Italian Beef 52

Lamb & Chickpeas 53

Lamb with Broccoli & Carrots 54

Braised Lamb with Vegetables 56

Rosemary Lamb 58

Mediterranean Lamb Meatballs 59

Chapter 8: Poultry Recipes 60

Chicken & Tofu 60

Chicken & Peanut Stir-Fry 62

Honey Mustard Chicken 63

Lemon Garlic Turkey 64

Chicken & Spinach 65

Balsamic Chicken 66

Greek Chicken Lettuce Wraps 67

Lemon Chicken with Kale 69

Chapter 9: Vegetarian Recipes 70

Kale & Tofu Salad	70
Boiled Potatoes with Tomato Salsa	72
Braised Summer Squash	73
Grilled Potatoes in a Packet	74
Mixed Greens Salad	75
Roasted Carrots	76
Porcini Mushrooms & Eggplant	77
Kale with Miso & Ginger	78
Grilled Zucchini with Tomato Relish	79
Cucumber Salad with Pesto	80

Chapter 10: Side Recipes 81

Fried Okra	81
Grilled Sweet Potatoes	82
Zucchini Fries	83
French Green Beans	84
Roasted Summer Squash	85
Veggie Mash	86
Mushroom Medley	87
Mustard Potatoes	88

Chapter 11: Fish and Seafood Recipes 89

Grilled Salmon with Ginger Sauce	89
Almond Crusted Baked Chili Mahi Mahi	90
Swordfish with Tomato Salsa	92
Salmon & Asparagus	93
Halibut with Spicy Apricot Sauce	94
Popcorn Shrimp	95
Shrimp Lemon Kebab	96

    Grilled Herbed Salmon with Raspberry Sauce & Cucumber Dill Dip 97

    Tarragon Scallops 98

    Garlic Shrimp & Spinach 99

Chapter 12: Dessert Recipes 100

    Chocolate & Raspberry Ice Cream 100

    Mocha Pops 101

    Choco Banana Bites 102

    Blueberries with Yogurt 103

    Fruit Kebab 104

    Roasted Mangoes 105

    Figs with Yogurt 106

    Grilled Peaches 107

    Fruit Salad 108

    Strawberry & Watermelon Pops 109

Conclusion 110

Introduction

Did you know that about 1.5 million American adults are diagnosed with diabetes each year?

In the 1980s, only 108 million cases were reported.

This has risen to 422 million in 2014.

In 2016, more than 1.6 million deaths were caused directly by this condition while over 2 million were due to high blood sugar.

All these figures from the World Health Organization show you that diabetes is not something to be taken lightly.

Diabetes, which is a primary cause of stroke, heart attack, kidney failure, lower limb amputation and blindness, is one of the most serious medical conditions that threatens the health and life of many people all over the world.

This is why, medical experts are developing preventive measures, management procedures and treatments for people who suffer from diabetes.

Aside from these, many experts recommend proper diet along with regular exercise to help manage the condition more efficiently.

In this book, we will discuss the process on how to prepare proper diet if you are someone who has been diagnosed with diabetes.

The recipes that you will find in this book are not only ideal for those with diabetes, but are also easy and simple to prepare. This way, even if you do not have much time to spare, you do not have to worry about it.

Not to mention, these recipes are also delicious and appetizing.

After all, living with diabetes does not mean that you can no longer enjoy delicious food.

It is just a matter of proper food preparation.

Chapter 1: Understanding Diabetes

What is Diabetes?

Diabetes refers to a chronic disease that takes place when either of the two happens:

- The pancreas is unable to produce sufficient insulin
- The body is not able to use or process the insulin that it produces

Insulin is the hormone responsible for regulating blood sugar.
Hyperglycemia is a condition in which the blood sugar level is elevated, and over time, may cause serious damage to many of the systems of the body including the blood vessels and the nerves.

Types of Diabetes

Diabetes is an umbrella term for different types of insulin-related medical conditions. Most people use diabetes to refer to type 2 diabetes, but there are actually many different forms.

Here are the different types of diabetes:

Type-1 Diabetes

Formerly known as insulin-dependent or juvenile diabetes, type-1 diabetes occurs when the body is unable to produce sufficient amount of insulin.
People diagnosed with this condition are required to administer insulin into their bodies daily.
The cause of type 1 diabetes is not known.

It is also not preventable, according to medical experts.

About 10 percent of diabetes cases are attributed to type-1 diabetes.

Type 2 Diabetes

The most common form of diabetes is type-2 diabetes, which accounts for almost 90 percent of all cases.

Previously referred to as non-insulin-dependent or adult-onset diabetes, this one is characterized by the body's inability to properly use insulin.

This is primarily caused by excessive weight and sedentary lifestyle.

Many people who are overweight and obese are at great risk of this condition.

In the past, this particular type of diabetes was only experienced by adults hence the former name adult-onset diabetes. But now, it is occurring more and more often among children.

Gestational Diabetes

Gestational diabetes refers to hyperglycemia with blood sugar levels elevating above normal but still below the diagnostic level for diabetes, and occurs during pregnancy.

Women who are diagnosed with this type of diabetes are at risk of various complications not only during pregnancy but also during delivery.

Women with this condition and their children are at increased risk of type 2 diabetes.

This is often diagnosed during prenatal screening.

Impaired Glucose Tolerance and Impaired Fasting Glycemia

These two conditions: impaired glucose tolerance and impaired fasting glycemia are conditions precursor to diabetes.

People who suffer from these two conditions are at great risk of type 2 diabetes.

How to Identify if you have Diabetes

The early signs of diabetes include:

- Hunger and fatigue

When your body consumes food, it converts it into glucose so that the cells can use it for energy. The body needs insulin so that the cells can take in the glucose. Without enough insulin or if the cells are unable to use insulin, the body does not get any energy, making you feel tired as well as hungry all the time.

- Excessive thirst and urination

Usually, a person pees from four to seven times in a day. But with people who suffer from diabetes pee a lot more. This also makes you thirsty more frequently.

- Dry mouth and itchy skin

When the body uses fluids to create urine, it has less moisture to keep the mouth and skin from drying.

- Blurry vision

Changes in the body's fluid levels can inflame the lens of the eyes, making it more difficult for the eyes to focus.

Symptoms of type-2 diabetes include:

- Yeast infections
- Slow healing wounds
- Pain in the muscles
- Numbness of legs and feet

Symptoms of type-1 diabetes are the following:

- Unexplained weight loss
- Nausea and vomiting

As for gestational diabetes, there are no symptoms. The condition is only determined during prenatal screening.

Risk Factors

Enumerated below are the risk factors for three different types of diabetes:

Risk Factors for Type-1 Diabetes

As mentioned earlier, the exact cause of this type of diabetes is not known. However, several factors have been found to increase its risk and these include:

- Family history

You are at an increased risk of type-1 diabetes when you have a parent or sibling suffering from this condition.

- Viral infections

Certain viral infections have been found to increase risk of this type of diabetes.

- Presence of antibodies

Certain types of antibodies have been linked to type-1 diabetes. But it is not guaranteed that you will develop this condition if you have these antibodies.

- Geographical location

It has been found in studies that type-1 diabetes is more frequent in certain countries such as Sweden and Finland.

Risk Factors for Type-2 Diabetes

People who fit the following descriptions are at increased risk of type-2 diabetes:

- Overweight or obese

Experts say that the fattier tissue there is in your body, the more difficult it is for the cells to use insulin.

- Inactive

People who live sedentary lifestyle are more prone to have excessive weight. Plus, physical activity also helps the cells make use of insulin.

- Have family suffering from this condition

As with type-1 diabetes, you have greater risk for type-2 diabetes when anyone in your family is diagnosed with this condition.

- Elderly

The risk for type-2 diabetes is greater for older people.

Risk Factors for Gestational Diabetes

Any woman who is carrying a baby may possibly develop this type of diabetes but it is more commonly seen among the following:

- Women who are older than 25
- Women who have personal or family history

- Women who are overweight or obese
- Women who are black, Asian, Hispanic or American Indian

The Link between Obesity and Type 2 Diabetes

As discussed previously, excessive weight and obesity are a common risk factor for type 2 diabetes.

Experts explain that people who are overweight or obese are more prone to develop this type of diabetes.

When you are overweight, the cells of your fat tissues need to process a lot more nutrients than normal.

The cells then become overly stressed which in turn triggers inflammation that produces a protein known as cytokines.

The cytokines block the signals sent by the insulin receptors, gradually resulting in the insulin resistance of the cells.

Once the cells become resistant to insulin, they are no longer able to convert glucose into energy, causing a spike in the blood sugar level.

A common complication is the inflammation of cells that lead to heart disease.

How can Diabetes be Prevented and Controlled

Here are the ways on how to prevent diabetes:

- Limit intake of sugar and refined carbs

Studies have shown the link between excessive consumption of foods rich in sugar and refined carbs and the risk of diabetes.

- Exercise regularly

This will help maintain the sensitivity of cells to insulin.

- Drink water

The best way to keep yourself hydrated is with water. Other than this, it also reduces the risk of diabetes than when you regularly consume soda and other sugary drinks.

- Lose weight

Since obesity is linked to type-2 diabetes, it is best to go on a weight loss program to start shedding unwanted pounds.

- Quit smoking

Smoking can lead to many health problems including lung cancer, heart disease and so on. It has also been found to increase the risk of diabetes by up to 44 percent.

- Take in enough vitamin D

Vitamin D is a nutrient responsible for controlling blood sugar levels. You are more likely to develop diabetes if you are deficient in this vitamin.

- Consume less processed foods

Minimize consumption of processed foods to reduce the risk of diabetes.

- Drink tea

Studies have found that regular consumption of green tea can help prevent the onset of diabetes.

As for living with this condition, here are some techniques that will help you control your blood sugar levels:

- Follow a low-carb diet

Low carb diets can help you manage your condition more efficiently.

- Eat small portions

It is better for anyone living with diabetes to consume small portions of food and to avoid large meals. Break down your meals into smaller portions throughout the day.

- Get regular exercise

Regular exercise is necessary to help maintain proper blood sugar levels. Moderate exercise of at least 30 minutes each day is recommended for people diagnosed with this condition.

- Consume foods high in fiber

A high fiber diet is good for both the gut health and management of weight. Not only that, this also lowers blood sugar levels.

A Healthy Meal Can Help Ease the Effects of Diabetes

It has been proven that there is a strong link between diet and diabetes.
Experts confirm that people diagnosed with diabetes who maintain diets that are rich in refined carbs, sugar and fats suffer more from complications and problems than those who adopt healthier diet programs.
If you have been diagnosed with diabetes, it is imperative to start implementing a healthy diet—one that is low in calories, fat, sugar, and refined carbs, and one that focuses primarily on whole grains, fruits, vegetables, high fiber and nutritious foods.

Food to Eat

Some of the best foods to consume when you have diabetes include:

- Fatty fish (salmon, sardines, anchovies, mackerel, herring)
- Leafy vegetables (spinach, kale)
- Cinnamon
- Eggs
- Turmeric
- Greek yogurt
- Nuts (almonds, Brazil nuts, cashews, hazelnuts, pecans, walnuts)
- Seeds (flaxseeds, sunflower seeds, chia seeds)
- Broccoli
- Squash
- Asparagus
- Olive oil
- Apple cider vinegar
- Fruits and berries
- Spices (garlic, onion)
- Herbs (both dried and fresh)

Food to Avoid

Some of the foods and beverages that you should stay away from when you have diabetes include:

- Sugary beverages
- Foods rich in trans fats

- White bread
- White rice
- White pasta
- Fruit flavored yogurt
- Sweetened cereals
- Coffee
- Agave nectar
- Dried fruits
- Candies
- Cookies and pastries
- Packaged snacks
- Fruit juice
- French fries

Chapter 2: Why Meal Prep?

Whether you are too busy to cook or you are someone with special dietary requirements, meal prep can help you maintain a healthier lifestyle.

Meal planning also helps you achieve the following:

1. Save time

When you have your meals prepared beforehand, you won't have to spend time thinking about what to eat, do the grocery, and cook food on that day. Instead, you can use the time you save on exercising and other activities that contribute to your well-being.

2. Save money

One of the major benefits of meal prep is the monetary savings. For one, buying in bulk helps you reduce overall food costs. It's also cheaper to cook at home than to eat out, which is what usually happens when you're hungry and have no time for food preparation.

3. Stay on top of your goals

Do you need to watch your carb intake? Or, do you just want to ensure that you're eating nutritionally balanced whole foods? Whatever the reason, meal prepping helps you stay on track and makes achieving your goals much more manageable.

4. Control your portions

Part of meal prep is portion control as it entails planning how much food you have to cook for a certain number of meals. Placing food in individual containers allows for both controlling portions as well as the ease of having food you can easily bring on the go.

5. Manage hunger

Having your food already prepared helps you stave off hunger pangs so you won't be tempted to eat out or make unwise food choices. For diabetics, having a meal that you can eat whenever you feel hungry is necessary to keep your blood sugar levels normal.

You've learned some of the reasons why you need to plan and prepare your meals ahead of time. However, before you start rushing out to do your grocery, you need to know some of the common mistakes related to meal prep in the next chapter.

Chapter 3: The Common Mistakes by Meal Prepping Beginners

To take advantage of the benefits meal planning has to offer, make sure you avoid the following mistakes:

Mistake # 1 - Not tailoring your meal plan according to your unique needs

It's now very easy to prep meals. You can even download meal plans right to your smartphone or tablet so you won't have to do the planning yourself. Unfortunately, this could cause some problems especially if you have special dietary requirements. Therefore, before you start making a grocery list, talk to your doctor or a nutritionist who can help you tailor your meal plan based on your specific needs.

For those with diabetes, the American Diabetes Association provides general dietary guidelines on their website, although it is still best that you contact a certified diabetes educator or a registered dietician who can keep track of your individual progress and recommend adjustments, if needed.

Mistake # 2 - Not preparing balanced meals

Whether they are diabetic or not, many people make the mistake of having too much of one or two food groups while neglecting the others. While you can't have too much carbohydrates if you have diabetes or if you're on a certain weight loss plan, carbs are a necessary part of a healthy diet and should be a component of every balanced meal.

On the other hand, just because fats don't have a direct effect on blood glucose levels doesn't mean you can eat too much. Fatty foods can slow down digestion and make it even more difficult for the insulin in your body to do its work. It also increases the risk of cardiovascular problems.

Mistake # 3 - Doing all your meal prep once a week

Weekends are ideal for prepping meals for the whole week. However, if you prepare all your meals for the next six days on Sunday, for example, the meals that you eat towards the end of the week either don't taste good or have already spoiled. This is why it's best to do your meal prep twice: once on the weekend and another in the middle of the week.

Mistake # 4 - Not storing your food properly

Improper storage is another common cause of food spoilage. Thus, it is important to use the appropriate container for each type of food. Where you put your pre-prepared meals is also something to consider.

Make sure to place the food in a refrigerator that is kept below 40 degrees Fahrenheit. Of course, following food safety practices in the food prep area is essential to avoid cross contamination and food poisoning.

Chapter 4: The Benefits of the Diabetes Meal Prep

Meal planning is extremely helpful in many practical ways, but one of its greatest benefits is on a person's health, particularly if it combines healthy balanced food and proper portion control.

Benefit # 1 - It helps improve your general health

Whether or not you have a medical condition, meal planning can help you improve your overall health when the meals provide all the macro and micronutrients your body needs. It also helps you avoid saturated fats and processed sugars, which is what most people would reach for if they're hungry and just want something satisfying.

Benefit # 2 - It ensures that you can eat on time

As mentioned in Chapter 2, preparing your meals in advance helps manage hunger pains. Missing a meal or delaying it can cause your blood sugar level to drop too low, a condition otherwise known as hypoglycemia.
Hypoglycemia can cause shaking, disorientation, and irritability. You may even have a seizure if your blood sugar level gets any lower. Having your meal already prepared ensures that you can always eat on time and, therefore, decrease the risk of low blood glucose.

Benefit # 3 - It lowers your risk of heart disease

Diabetes increases the risk of heart disease. With the help of a dietician, planning your meals can help you reduce this risk. Because meal prep reduces the time you need to spend in the kitchen, you'll have more opportunities to exercise and do other activities that promote a healthier lifestyle.

Benefit # 4 - It lowers your risk of cancer

Diabetes also increases the risk of all forms of cancer. While experts are still unable to identify the exact link between these two conditions, they expect that it has something to do with insulin resistance and obesity. Cancer patients are advised to pursue a healthy lifestyle, which includes eating a balanced diet and getting adequate exercise. Because these activities are also encouraged among diabetics, the risk of cancer is lowered.

Benefit # 5 - It helps you maintain healthy body weight

Again, portion control plays a part in this area. Even if you eat healthy food, over-indulging can lead to an unhealthy weight gain, which can make it harder to control your blood sugar level.

If left unchecked, this could lead to high blood sugar levels or hyperglycemia, which can cause various complications that include heart and liver damage as well as loss of kidney function.

It's important to note that while meal planning can help keep the effects of diabetes under control, you and your dietician still need to conduct a periodic review of its effectiveness and make changes whenever necessary.

Chapter 5: 30-Day Meal Plan

Day 1

Breakfast: Whole Grain Cereal

Lunch: Pork Chops with Grape Sauce

Dinner: Grilled Salmon with Ginger Sauce

Day 2

Breakfast: Vegetable Omelet

Lunch: Chicken and Peanut Stir-Fry

Dinner: Almond Crusted Baked Chili Mahi Mahi

Day 3

Breakfast: Granola with Fruits

Lunch: Salmon and Asparagus

Dinner: Braised Lamb with Vegetables

Day 4

Breakfast: Sausage, Egg and Potatoes

Lunch: Kale with Miso and Ginger

Dinner: Shrimp Lemon Kebab

Day 5

Breakfast: Apple and Cinnamon Pancake

Lunch: Chicken and Tofu

Dinner: Italian Beef

Day 6

Breakfast: Yogurt Breakfast Pudding

Lunch: Mixed Greens Salad

Dinner: Swordfish with Tomato Salsa

Day 7

Breakfast: Granola with Fruits

Lunch: Pork Chops with Grape Sauce

Dinner: Cucumber Salad with Pesto

Day 8

Breakfast: Oatmeal with Mango Slices

Lunch: Honey Mustard Chicken

Dinner: Kale & Tofu Salad

Day 9

Breakfast: Cucumber and Yogurt

Lunch: Rosemary Lamb

Dinner: Salmon and Asparagus

Day 10

Breakfast: Almonds and Fruits

Lunch: Sesame Pork with Mustard Sauce

Dinner: Halibut with Spicy Apricot Sauce

Day 11

Breakfast: Apple & Cinnamon Pancake

Lunch: Grilled Zucchini with Tomato Relish

Dinner: Salmon with Ginger Sauce

Day 12

Breakfast: Oatmeal with Banana Cubes

Lunch: Braised Summer Squash

Dinner: Lamb with Broccoli & Carrots

Day 13

Breakfast: Gluten Free Pancake with Fruits

Lunch: Lemon Garlic Turkey

Dinner: Porcini Mushrooms & Eggplant

Day 14

Breakfast: Granola with Fruits

Lunch: Popcorn Shrimp

Dinner: Kale with Miso & Ginger

Day 15

Breakfast: Asparagus and Cheese Omelet

Lunch: Lamb and Chickpeas

Dinner: Braised Summer Squash

Day 16

Breakfast: Almond and Berry Smoothie

Lunch: Irish Pork Roast

Dinner: Chicken and Spinach

Day 17

Breakfast: Boiled Eggs and Ham

Lunch: Italian Beef

Dinner: Shrimp Lemon Kebab

Day 18

Breakfast: Breakfast Parfait

Lunch: Boiled Potatoes with Tomato Salsa

Dinner: Beef and Asparagus

Day 19

Breakfast: Cucumber and Yogurt

Lunch: Pork Chops with Grape Sauce

Dinner: Halibut with Spicy Apricot Sauce

Day 20

Breakfast: Sausage, Egg and Potatoes

Lunch: Almond Crusted Baked Chili Mahi Mahi

Dinner: Balsamic Chicken

Day 21

Breakfast: Breakfast Burrito

Lunch: Grilled Salmon with Ginger Sauce

Dinner: Mediterranean Lamb Meatballs

Day 22

Breakfast: Yogurt Breakfast Pudding

Lunch: Barbecue Beef Brisket

Dinner: Greek Chicken Lettuce Wraps

Day 23

Breakfast: Spinach Scramble

Lunch: Porcini Mushrooms and Eggplant

Dinner: Grilled Herbed Salmon with Raspberry Sauce and Cucumber Dill Dip

Day 24

Breakfast: Apple and Cinnamon Pancake

Lunch: Roasted Pork and Apples

Dinner: Swordfish with Tomato Salsa

Day 25

Breakfast: Almond and Berry Smoothie

Lunch: Tarragon Scallops

Dinner: Steak with Tomato & Herbs

Day 26

Breakfast: Vegetable Omelet

Lunch: Lemon Chicken with Kale

Dinner: Kale and Tofu Salad

Day 27

Breakfast: Muesli

Lunch: Grilled Zucchini with Tomato Relish

Dinner: Tarragon Scallops

Day 28

Breakfast: Breakfast Parfait

Lunch: Halibut with Spicy Apricot Sauce

Dinner: Cucumber Salad with Pesto

Day 29

Breakfast: Scrambled Eggs with Tomato and Onion

Lunch: Grilled Herbed Salmon with Raspberry Sauce and Cucumber Dill Dip

Dinner: Steak with Mushroom Sauce

Day 30

Breakfast: Spinach Scramble

Lunch: Garlic Shrimp and Spinach

Dinner: Pork with Cranberry Relish

Chapter 6: Breakfast

Granola with Fruits

Preparation Time: 15 minutes
Cooking Time: 35 minutes
Servings: 6

Ingredients:

- 3 cups quick cooking oats
- 1 cup almonds, sliced
- ½ cup wheat germ
- 3 tablespoons butter
- 1 teaspoon ground cinnamon
- 1 cup honey
- 3 cups whole grain cereal flakes
- ½ cup raisins
- ½ cup dried cranberries
- ½ cup dates, pitted and chopped

Method:

1. Preheat your oven to 325 degrees F.
2. Arrange the almonds and oats on a baking sheet.
3. Bake for 15 minutes.
4. Mix the wheat germ, butter, cinnamon and honey in a bowl.
5. Add the toasted almonds and oats.
6. Mix well.
7. Spread on the baking sheet.
8. Bake for 20 minutes.
9. Mix with the rest of the ingredients.
10. Let cool and serve.

Nutritional Value:

- Calories 210
- Total Fat 7 g
- Saturated Fat 2 g
- Cholesterol 5 mg
- Sodium 58 mg
- Total Carbohydrate 36 g
- Dietary Fiber 4 g
- Total Sugars 2 g
- Protein 5 g
- Potassium 250 mg

Apple & Cinnamon Pancake

Preparation Time: 15 minutes
Cooking Time: 10 minutes
Servings: 4

Ingredients:

- ¼ teaspoon ground cinnamon
- 1 ¾ cups Better Baking Mix
- 1 tablespoon oil
- 1 cup water
- 2 egg whites
- ½ cup sugar-free applesauce
- Cooking spray
- 1 cup plain yogurt
- Sugar substitute

Method:

1. Blend the cinnamon and the baking mix in a bowl.
2. Create a hole in the middle and add the oil, water, egg and applesauce.
3. Mix well.
4. Spray your pan with oil.
5. Place it on medium heat.
6. Pour ¼ cup of the batter.
7. Flip the pancake and cook until golden.
8. Serve with yogurt and sugar substitute.

Nutritional Value:

- Calories 231
- Total Fat 6 g
- Saturated Fat 1 g
- Cholesterol 54 mg
- Sodium 545 mg
- Total Carbohydrate 37 g
- Dietary Fiber 4 g
- Total Sugars 1 g
- Protein 8 g
- Potassium 750 mg

Spinach Scramble

Preparation Time: 5 minutes
Cooking Time: 15 minutes
Servings: 2

Ingredients:

- ¼ cup liquid egg substitute
- ¼ cup skim milk
- Salt and pepper to taste
- 2 tablespoons crumbled bacon
- 13 ½ oz. canned spinach, drained
- Cooking spray

Method:

1. Mix all the ingredients in a large bowl.
2. Pour the mixture on a pan greased with oil, placed over medium heat.
3. Stir until fully cooked.
4. Calories: 70 calories, Carbohydrates: 5 g, Protein: 8 g, Fat: 2 g, Saturated Fat: 1 g, Sodium: 700 mg, Fiber: 2 g

Nutritional Value:

- Calories 70
- Total Fat 2 g
- Saturated Fat 1 g
- Cholesterol 25 mg
- Sodium 700 mg
- Total Carbohydrate 5 g
- Dietary Fiber 2 g
- Total Sugars 1 g
- Protein 8 g
- Potassium 564 mg

Breakfast Parfait

Preparation Time: 5 minutes
Cooking Time: 0 minute
Servings: 2

Ingredients:

- 4 oz. unsweetened applesauce
- 6 oz. non-fat and sugar-free vanilla yogurt
- ¼ teaspoon pumpkin pie spice
- ¼ teaspoon honey
- 1 cup low-fat granola

Method:

1. Mix all the ingredients except the granola in a bowl.
2. Layer the mixture with the granola in a cup.
3. Refrigerate before serving.

Nutritional Value:

- Calories 287
- Total Fat 3 g
- Saturated Fat 1 g
- Cholesterol 28 mg
- Sodium 186 mg
- Total Carbohydrate 57 g
- Dietary Fiber 4 g
- Total Sugars 2 g
- Protein 8 g
- Potassium 450 mg

Asparagus & Cheese Omelet

Preparation Time: 10 minutes
Cooking Time: 10 minutes
Servings: 2

Ingredients:

- Cooking spray
- 4 spears asparagus, sliced
- Pepper to taste
- 3 egg whites
- ½ teaspoon olive oil
- 1 oz. spreadable cheese, sliced
- 1 teaspoon parsley, chopped

Method:

1. Spray oil on your pan.
2. Cook asparagus on the pan over medium high heat for 5 to 7 minutes.
3. Wrap with foil and set aside.
4. In a bowl, mix pepper and egg whites.
5. Add olive oil to the pan.
6. Add the egg whites.
7. When you start to see the sides forming, add the asparagus and cheese on top.
8. Use a spatula to lift and fold the egg.
9. Sprinkle parsley on top before serving.

Nutritional Value:

- Calories 119
- Total Fat 5 g
- Saturated Fat 2 g
- Cholesterol 10 mg
- Sodium 427 mg
- Total Carbohydrate 5 g
- Dietary Fiber 2 g
- Total Sugars 3 g
- Protein 15 g
- Potassium 308 mg

Sausage, Egg & Potatoes

Preparation Time: 15 minutes
Cooking Time: 10 hours and 10 minutes
Servings: 6

Ingredients:

- Cooking spray
- 12 oz. chicken sausage links, sliced
- 1 onion, sliced into wedges
- 2 red sweet peppers, sliced into strips
- 1 ½ lb. potatoes, sliced into strips
- ¼ cup low-sodium chicken broth
- Black pepper to taste
- ½ teaspoon dried thyme, crushed
- 6 eggs
- ½ cup low-fat cheddar cheese, shredded

Method:

1. Spray oil on a heavy foil sheet.
2. Put the sausage, onion, sweet peppers and potatoes on the foil.
3. Drizzle top with the chicken broth.
4. Season with the pepper and thyme.
5. Fold to seal.
6. Place the packet inside a cooker.
7. Cook on low setting for 10 hours.
8. Meanwhile, boil the egg until fully cooked.
9. Serve eggs with the sausage mixture.

Nutritional Value:

- Calories 281
- Total Fat 12 g
- Saturated Fat 4 g
- Cholesterol 262 mg
- Sodium 485 mg
- Total Carbohydrate 23 g
- Dietary Fiber 3 g
- Total Sugars 3 g
- Protein 21 g
- Potassium 262 mg

Cucumber & Yogurt

Preparation Time: 5 minutes
Cooking Time: 0 minute
Servings: 1

Ingredients:

- 1 cup low-fat yogurt
- ½ cup cucumber, diced
- ¼ teaspoon lemon zest
- ¼ teaspoon lemon juice
- ¼ teaspoon fresh mint, chopped
- Salt to taste

Method:

1. Mix all the ingredients in a jar.
2. Refrigerate and serve.

Nutritional Value:

- Calories 164
- Total Fat 4 g
- Saturated Fat 2 g
- Cholesterol 15 mg
- Sodium 318 mg
- Total Carbohydrate 19 g
- Dietary Fiber 1 g
- Total Sugars 18 g
- Protein 13 g
- Potassium 683 mg

Yogurt Breakfast Pudding

Preparation Time: 8 hours and 10 minutes
Cooking Time: 0 minute
Servings: 2

Ingredients:

- ½ cup rolled oats
- 6 oz. low-fat yogurt
- ¼ cup canned pineapple
- ½ cup fat-free milk
- ½ teaspoon vanilla
- ⅛ teaspoon ground cinnamon
- 1 tablespoon flaxseed meal
- 4 teaspoons almonds, toasted and sliced
- ½ cup apple, chopped

Method:

1. In a bowl, mix all the ingredients except almonds and apple.
2. Transfer the mixture into an airtight container.
3. Cover with the lid and refrigerate for 8 hours.
4. Top with the almonds and apple before serving.

Nutritional Value:

- Calories 255
- Total Fat 7 g
- Saturated Fat 1 g
- Cholesterol 5 mg
- Sodium 84 mg
- Total Carbohydrate 38 g
- Dietary Fiber 5 g
- Total Sugars 21 g
- Protein 11 g
- Potassium 345 mg

Vegetable Omelet

Preparation Time: 5 minutes
Cooking Time: 25 minutes
Servings: 4

Ingredients:

- ½ cup yellow summer squash, chopped
- ½ cup canned diced tomatoes with herbs, drained
- ½ ripe avocado, pitted and chopped
- ½ cup cucumber, chopped
- 2 eggs
- 2 tablespoons water
- Salt and pepper to taste
- 1 teaspoon dried basil, crushed
- Cooking spray
- ¼ cup low-fat Monterey Jack cheese, shredded
- Chives, chopped

Method:

1. In a bowl, mix the squash, tomatoes, avocado and cucumber.
2. In another bowl, mix the eggs, water, salt, pepper and basil.
3. Spray oil on a pan over medium heat.
4. Pour egg mixture on the pan.
5. Put the vegetable mixture on top of the egg.
6. Lift and fold.
7. Cook until the egg has set.
8. Sprinkle cheese and chives on top.

Nutritional Value:

- Calories 128
- Total Fat 6 g
- Saturated Fat 2 g
- Cholesterol 97 mg
- Sodium 357 mg
- Total Carbohydrate 7 g
- Dietary Fiber 3 g
- Total Sugars 4 g
- Protein 12 g
- Potassium 341 mg

Almond & Berry Smoothie

Preparation Time: 10 minutes
Cooking Time: 0 minute
Serving: 1

Ingredients:

- ⅔ cup frozen raspberries
- ½ cup frozen banana, sliced
- ½ cup almond milk (unsweetened)
- 3 tablespoons almonds, sliced
- ¼ teaspoon ground cinnamon
- ⅛ teaspoon vanilla extract
- ¼ cup blueberries
- 1 tablespoon coconut flakes (unsweetened)

Method:

1. Put all the ingredients in a blender except coconut flakes. Pulse until smooth.
2. Top with the coconut flakes before serving.

Nutritional Value:

- Calories 360
- Total Fat 19 g
- Saturated Fat 3 g
- Cholesterol 0 mg
- Sodium 89 mg
- Total Carbohydrate 46 g
- Dietary Fiber 14 g
- Total Sugars 21 g
- Protein 9 g
- Potassium 736 mg

Chapter 7: Meat Recipes

Pork Chops with Grape Sauce

Preparation Time: 15 minutes
Cooking Time: 25 minutes
Servings: 4

Ingredients:

- Cooking spray
- 4 pork chops
- ¼ cup onion, sliced
- 1 clove garlic, minced
- ½ cup low-sodium chicken broth
- ¾ cup apple juice
- 1 tablespoon cornstarch
- 1 tablespoon balsamic vinegar
- 1 teaspoon honey
- 1 cup seedless red grapes, sliced in half

Method:

1. Spray oil on your pan.
2. Put it over medium heat.
3. Add the pork chops to the pan.
4. Cook for 5 minutes per side.
5. Remove and set aside.
6. Add onion and garlic.
7. Cook for 2 minutes.
8. Pour in the broth and apple juice.
9. Bring to a boil.
10. Reduce heat to simmer.
11. Put the pork chops back to the skillet.
12. Simmer for 4 minutes.
13. In a bowl, mix the cornstarch, vinegar and honey.
14. Add to the pan.
15. Cook until the sauce has thickened.

16. Add the grapes.
17. Pour sauce over the pork chops before serving.

Nutritional Value:

- Calories 188
- Total Fat 4 g
- Saturated Fat 1 g
- Cholesterol 47 mg
- Sodium 117 mg
- Total Carbohydrate 18 g
- Dietary Fiber 1 g
- Total Sugars 13 g
- Protein 19 g
- Potassium 759 mg

Roasted Pork & Apples

Preparation Time: 15 minutes
Cooking Time: 30 minutes
Servings: 4

Ingredients:

- Salt and pepper to taste
- ½ teaspoon dried, crushed
- 1 lb. pork tenderloin
- 1 tablespoon canola oil
- 1 onion, sliced into wedges
- 3 cooking apples, sliced into wedges
- ⅔ cup apple cider
- Sprigs fresh sage

Method:

1. In a bowl, mix salt, pepper and sage.
2. Season both sides of pork with this mixture.
3. Place a pan over medium heat.
4. Brown both sides.
5. Transfer to a roasting pan.
6. Add the onion on top and around the pork.
7. Drizzle oil on top of the pork and apples.
8. Roast in the oven at 425 degrees F for 10 minutes.
9. Add the apples, roast for another 15 minutes.
10. In a pan, boil the apple cider and then simmer for 10 minutes.
11. Pour the apple cider sauce over the pork before serving.

Nutritional Value:

- Calories 239
- Total Fat 6 g
- Saturated Fat 1 g
- Cholesterol 74 mg
- Sodium 209 mg
- Total Carbohydrate 22 g
- Dietary Fiber 3 g
- Total Sugars 16 g
- Protein 24 g
- Potassium 655 mg

Pork with Cranberry Relish

Preparation Time: 30 minutes
Cooking Time: 30 minutes
Servings: 4

Ingredients:

- 12 oz. pork tenderloin, fat trimmed and sliced crosswise
- Salt and pepper to taste
- ¼ cup all-purpose flour
- 2 tablespoons olive oil
- 1 onion, sliced thinly
- ¼ cup dried cranberries
- ¼ cup low-sodium chicken broth
- 1 tablespoon balsamic vinegar

Method:

1. Flatten each slice of pork using a mallet.
2. In a dish, mix the salt, pepper and flour.
3. Dip each pork slice into the flour mixture.
4. Add oil to a pan over medium high heat.
5. Cook pork for 3 minutes per side or until golden crispy.
6. Transfer to a serving plate and cover with foil.
7. Cook the onion in the pan for 4 minutes.
8. Stir in the rest of the ingredients.
9. Simmer until the sauce has thickened.

Nutritional Value:

- Calories 211
- Total Fat 9 g
- Saturated Fat 2 g
- Cholesterol 53 mg
- Sodium 116 mg
- Total Carbohydrate 15 g
- Dietary Fiber 1 g
- Total Sugars 6 g
- Protein 18 g
- Potassium 378 mg

Irish Pork Roast

Preparation Time: 40 minutes
Cooking Time: 1 hour
Servings: 8

Ingredients:

- 1 ½ lb. parsnips, peeled and sliced into small pieces
- 1 ½ lb. carrots, sliced into small pieces
- 3 tablespoons olive oil, divided
- 2 teaspoons fresh thyme leaves, divided
- Salt and pepper to taste
- 2 lb. pork loin roast
- 1 teaspoon honey
- 1 cup dry hard cider
- Applesauce

Method:

1. Preheat your oven to 400 degrees F.
2. Drizzle half of the oil over the parsnips and carrots.
3. Season with half of thyme, salt and pepper.
4. Arrange on a roasting pan.
5. Rub the pork with the remaining oil.
6. Season with the remaining thyme.
7. Season with salt and pepper.
8. Put it on the roasting pan on top of the vegetables.
9. Roast for 65 minutes.
10. Let cool before slicing.
11. Transfer the carrots and parsnips in a bowl and mix with honey.
12. Add the cider.
13. Place in a pan and simmer over low heat until the sauce has thickened.
14. Serve the pork with the vegetables and applesauce.

Nutritional Value:

- Calories 272
- Total Fat 8 g
- Saturated Fat 2 g
- Cholesterol 61 mg
- Sodium 327 mg
- Total Carbohydrate 23 g
- Dietary Fiber 6 g
- Total Sugars 10 g
- Protein 24 g
- Potassium 887 mg

Sesame Pork with Mustard Sauce

Preparation Time: 25 minutes
Cooking Time: 25 minutes
Servings: 4

Ingredients:

- 2 tablespoons low-sodium teriyaki sauce
- ¼ cup chili sauce
- 2 cloves garlic, minced
- 2 teaspoons ginger, grated
- 2 pork tenderloins
- 2 teaspoons sesame seeds
- ¼ cup low fat sour cream
- 1 teaspoon Dijon mustard
- Salt to taste
- 1 scallion, chopped

Method:

1. Preheat your oven to 425 degrees F.
2. Mix the teriyaki sauce, chili sauce, garlic and ginger.
3. Put the pork on a roasting pan.
4. Brush the sauce on both sides of the pork.
5. Bake in the oven for 15 minutes.
6. Brush with more sauce.
7. Top with sesame seeds.
8. Roast for 10 more minutes.
9. Mix the rest of the ingredients.
10. Serve the pork with mustard sauce.

Nutritional Value:

- Calories 135
- Total Fat 3 g
- Saturated Fat 1 g
- Cholesterol 56X mg
- Sodium 302 mg
- Total Carbohydrate 7 g
- Dietary Fiber 1 g
- Total Sugars 15 g
- Protein 20 g
- Potassium 755 mg

Steak with Mushroom Sauce

Preparation Time: 20 minutes
Cooking Time: 5 minutes
Servings: 4

Ingredients:

- 12 oz. sirloin steak, sliced and trimmed
- 2 teaspoons grilling seasoning
- 2 teaspoons oil
- 6 oz. broccoli, trimmed
- 2 cups frozen peas
- 3 cups fresh mushrooms, sliced
- 1 cup beef broth (unsalted)
- 1 tablespoon mustard
- 2 teaspoons cornstarch
- Salt to taste

Method:

1. Preheat your oven to 350 degrees F.
2. Season meat with grilling seasoning.
3. In a pan over medium high heat, cook the meat and broccoli for 4 minutes.
4. Sprinkle the peas around the steak.
5. Put the pan inside the oven and bake for 8 minutes.
6. Remove both meat and vegetables from the pan.
7. Add the mushrooms to the pan.
8. Cook for 3 minutes.
9. Mix the broth, mustard, salt and cornstarch.
10. Add to the mushrooms.
11. Cook for 1 minute.
12. Pour sauce over meat and vegetables before serving.

Nutritional Value:

- Calories 226
- Total Fat 6 g
- Saturated Fat 2 g
- Cholesterol 51 mg
- Sodium 356 mg
- Total Carbohydrate 16 g
- Dietary Fiber 5 g
- Total Sugars 6 g
- Protein 26 g
- Potassium 780 mg

Steak with Tomato & Herbs

Preparation Time: 30 minutes
Cooking Time: 30 minutes
Servings: 2

Ingredients:

- 8 oz. beef loin steak, sliced in half
- Salt and pepper to taste
- Cooking spray
- 1 teaspoon fresh basil, snipped
- ¼ cup green onion, sliced
- ½ cup tomato, chopped

Method:

1. Season the steak with salt and pepper.
2. Spray oil on your pan.
3. Put the pan over medium high heat.
4. Once hot, add the steaks.
5. Reduce heat to medium.
6. Cook for 10 to 13 minutes for medium, turning once.
7. Add the basil and green onion.
8. Cook for 2 minutes.
9. Add the tomato.
10. Cook for 1 minute.
11. Let cool a little before slicing.

Nutritional Value:

- Calories 170
- Total Fat 6 g
- Saturated Fat 2 g
- Cholesterol 66 mg
- Sodium 207 mg
- Total Carbohydrate 3 g
- Dietary Fiber 1 g
- Total Sugars 5 g
- Protein 25 g
- Potassium 477 mg

Barbecue Beef Brisket

Preparation Time: 25 minutes
Cooking Time: 10 hours
Servings: 10

Ingredients:

- 4 lb. beef brisket (boneless), trimmed and sliced
- 1 bay leaf
- 2 onions, sliced into rings
- ½ teaspoon dried thyme, crushed
- ¼ cup chili sauce
- 1 clove garlic, minced
- Salt and pepper to taste
- 2 tablespoons light brown sugar
- 2 tablespoons cornstarch
- 2 tablespoons cold water

Method:

1. Put the meat in a slow cooker.
2. Add the bay leaf and onion.
3. In a bowl, mix the thyme, chili sauce, salt, pepper and sugar.
4. Pour the sauce over the meat.
5. Mix well.
6. Seal the pot and cook on low heat for 10 hours.
7. Discard the bay leaf.
8. Pour cooking liquid in a pan.
9. Add the mixed water and cornstarch.
10. Simmer until the sauce has thickened.
11. Pour the sauce over the meat.

Nutritional Value:

- Calories 182
- Total Fat 6 g
- Saturated Fat 2 g
- Cholesterol 57 mg
- Sodium 217 mg
- Total Carbohydrate 9 g
- Dietary Fiber 1 g
- Total Sugars 4 g
- Protein 20 g
- Potassium 383 mg

Beef & Asparagus

Preparation Time: 15 minutes
Cooking Time: 10 minutes
Servings: 4

Ingredients:

- 2 teaspoons olive oil
- 1 lb. lean beef sirloin, trimmed and sliced
- 1 carrot, shredded
- Salt and pepper to taste
- 12 oz. asparagus, trimmed and sliced
- 1 teaspoon dried herbes de Provence, crushed
- ½ cup Marsala
- ¼ teaspoon lemon zest

Method:

1. Pour oil in a pan over medium heat.
2. Add the beef and carrot.
3. Season with salt and pepper.
4. Cook for 3 minutes.
5. Add the asparagus and herbs.
6. Cook for 2 minutes.
7. Add the Marsala and lemon zest.
8. Cook for 5 minutes, stirring frequently.

Nutritional Value:

- Calories 327
- Total Fat 7 g
- Saturated Fat 2 g
- Cholesterol 69 mg
- Sodium 209 mg
- Total Carbohydrate 29 g
- Dietary Fiber 2 g
- Total Sugars 3 g
- Protein 28 g
- Potassium 576 mg

Italian Beef

Preparation Time: 20 minutes
Cooking Time: 1 hour and 20 minutes
Servings: 4

Ingredients:

- Cooking spray
- 1 lb. beef round steak, trimmed and sliced
- 1 cup onion, chopped
- 2 cloves garlic, minced
- 1 cup green bell pepper, chopped
- ½ cup celery, chopped
- 2 cups mushrooms, sliced
- 14 ½ oz. canned diced tomatoes
- ½ teaspoon dried basil
- ¼ teaspoon dried oregano
- ⅛ teaspoon crushed red pepper
- 2 tablespoons Parmesan cheese, grated

Method:

1. Spray oil on the pan over medium heat.
2. Cook the meat until brown on both sides.
3. Transfer meat to a plate.
4. Add the onion, garlic, bell pepper, celery and mushroom to the pan.
5. Cook until tender.
6. Add the tomatoes, herbs, and pepper.
7. Put the meat back to the pan.
8. Simmer while covered for 1 hour and 15 minutes.
9. Stir occasionally.
10. Sprinkle Parmesan cheese on top of the dish before serving.

Nutritional Value:

- Calories 212
- Total Fat 4 g
- Saturated Fat 1 g
- Cholesterol 51 mg
- Sodium 296 mg
- Total Carbohydrate 14 g
- Dietary Fiber 3 g
- Total Sugars 6 g
- Protein 30 g
- Potassium 876 mg

Lamb & Chickpeas

Preparation Time: 30 minutes
Cooking Time: 30 minutes
Servings: 4

Ingredients:

- 1 lb. lamb leg (boneless), trimmed and sliced into small pieces
- 2 tablespoons olive oil
- 1 teaspoon ground coriander
- Salt and pepper to taste
- ½ teaspoon ground cumin
- ¼ teaspoon red pepper, crushed
- ¼ cup fresh mint, chopped
- 2 teaspoons lemon zest
- 2 cloves garlic, minced
- 30 oz. unsalted chickpeas, rinsed and drained
- 1 cup tomatoes, chopped
- 1 cup English cucumber, chopped
- ¼ cup fresh parsley, snipped
- 1 tablespoon red wine vinegar

Method:
1. Preheat your oven to 375 degrees F.
2. Place the lamb on a baking dish.
3. Toss in half of the following: oil, cumin and coriander.
4. Season with red pepper, salt and pepper.
5. Mix well.
6. Roast for 20 minutes.
7. In a bowl, combine the rest of the ingredients with the remaining seasonings.
8. Add salt and pepper.
9. Serve lamb with chickpea mixture.

Nutritional Value:

- Calories 366
- Total Fat 15 g
- Saturated Fat 3 g
- Cholesterol 74 mg
- Sodium 369 mg
- Total Carbohydrate 27 g
- Dietary Fiber 7 g
- Total Sugars 3 g
- Protein 32 g
- Potassium 579 mg

Lamb with Broccoli & Carrots

Preparation Time: 20 minutes
Cooking Time: 10 minutes
Servings: 4

Ingredients:

- 2 cloves garlic, minced
- 1 tablespoon fresh ginger, grated
- ¼ teaspoon red pepper, crushed
- 2 tablespoons low-sodium soy sauce
- 1 tablespoon white vinegar
- 1 tablespoon cornstarch
- 12 oz. lamb meat, trimmed and sliced
- 2 teaspoons cooking oil
- 1 lb. broccoli, sliced into florets
- 2 carrots, sliced into strips
- ¾ cup low-sodium beef broth
- 4 green onions, chopped
- 2 cups cooked spaghetti squash pasta

Method:

1. Combine the garlic, ginger, red pepper, soy sauce, vinegar and cornstarch in a bowl.
2. Add lamb to the marinade.
3. Marinate for 10 minutes.
4. Discard marinade.
5. In a pan over medium heat, add the oil.
6. Add the lamb and cook for 3 minutes.
7. Transfer lamb to a plate.
8. Add the broccoli and carrots.
9. Cook for 1 minute.
10. Pour in the beef broth.
11. Cook for 5 minutes.
12. Put the meat back to the pan.
13. Sprinkle with green onion and serve on top of spaghetti squash.

Nutritional Value:

- Calories 205
- Total Fat 6 g
- Saturated Fat 1 g
- Cholesterol 40 mg
- Sodium 659 mg
- Total Carbohydrate 17 g
- Dietary Fiber 4 g
- Total Sugars 3 g
- Protein 22 g
- Potassium 772 mg

Braised Lamb with Vegetables

Preparation Time: 30 minutes
Cooking Time: 2 hours and 15 minutes
Servings: 6

Ingredients:

- Salt and pepper to taste
- 2 ½ lb. boneless lamb leg, trimmed and sliced into cubes
- 1 tablespoon olive oil
- 1 onion, chopped
- 1 carrot, chopped
- 14 oz. canned diced tomatoes
- 1 cup low-sodium beef broth
- 1 tablespoon fresh rosemary, chopped
- 4 cloves garlic, minced
- 1 cup pearl onions
- 1 cup baby turnips, peeled and sliced into wedges
- 1 ½ cups baby carrots
- 1 ½ cups peas
- 2 tablespoons fresh parsley, chopped

Method:

1. Sprinkle salt and pepper on both sides of the lamb.
2. Pour oil in a deep skillet.
3. Cook the lamb for 6 minutes.
4. Transfer lamb to a plate.
5. Add onion and carrot.
6. Cook for 3 minutes.
7. Stir in the tomatoes, broth, rosemary and garlic.
8. Simmer for 5 minutes.
9. Add the lamb back to the skillet.
10. Reduce heat to low.
11. Simmer for 1 hour and 15 minutes.
12. Add the pearl onion, baby carrot and baby turnips.
13. Simmer for 30 minutes.
14. Add the peas.

15. Cook for 1 minute.
16. Garnish with parsley before serving.

Nutritional Value:

- Calories 420
- Total Fat 14 g
- Saturated Fat 4 g
- Cholesterol 126 mg
- Sodium 529 mg
- Total Carbohydrate 16 g
- Dietary Fiber 4 g
- Total Sugars 7 g
- Protein 43 g
- Potassium 988 mg

Rosemary Lamb

Preparation Time: 15 minutes
Cooking Time: 2 hours
Servings: 14

Ingredients:

- Salt and pepper to taste
- 2 teaspoons fresh rosemary, snipped
- 5 lb. whole leg of lamb, trimmed and cut with slits on all sides
- 3 cloves garlic, slivered
- 1 cup water

Method:

1. Preheat your oven to 375 degrees F.
2. Mix salt, pepper and rosemary in a bowl.
3. Sprinkle mixture all over the lamb.
4. Insert slivers of garlic into the slits.
5. Put the lamb on a roasting pan.
6. Add water to the pan.
7. Roast for 2 hours.

Nutritional Value:

- Calories 136
- Total Fat 4 g
- Saturated Fat 1 g
- Cholesterol 71 mg
- Sodium 218 mg
- Protein 23 g
- Potassium 248 mg

Mediterranean Lamb Meatballs

Preparation Time: 10 minutes
Cooking Time: 20 minutes
Servings: 8

Ingredients:

- 12 oz. roasted red peppers
- 1 ½ cups whole wheat breadcrumbs
- 2 eggs, beaten
- 1/3 cup tomato sauce
- ½ cup fresh basil
- ¼ cup parsley, snipped
- Salt and pepper to taste
- 2 lb. lean ground lamb

Method:

1. Preheat your oven to 350 degrees F.
2. In a bowl, mix all the ingredients and then form into meatballs.
3. Put the meatballs on a baking pan.
4. Bake in the oven for 20 minutes.

Nutritional Value:

- Calories 94
- Total Fat 3 g
- Saturated Fat 1 g
- Cholesterol 35 mg
- Sodium 170 mg
- Total Carbohydrate 2 g
- Dietary Fiber 1 g
- Total Sugars 0 g
- Protein 14 g
- Potassium 266 mg

Chapter 8: Poultry Recipes

Chicken & Tofu

Preparation Time: 1 hour and 15 minutes
Cooking Time: 25 minutes
Servings: 6

Ingredients:

- 2 tablespoons olive oil, divided
- 2 tablespoons orange juice
- 1 tablespoon Worcestershire sauce
- 1 tablespoon low-sodium soy sauce
- 1 teaspoon ground turmeric
- 1 teaspoon dry mustard
- 8 oz. chicken breast, cooked and sliced into cubes
- 8 oz. extra-firm tofu, drained and sliced into cubed
- 2 carrots, sliced into thin strips
- 1 cup mushroom, sliced
- 2 cups fresh bean sprouts
- 3 green onions, sliced
- 1 red sweet pepper, sliced into strips

Method:

1. In a bowl, mix half of the oil with the orange juice, Worcestershire sauce, soy sauce, turmeric and mustard.
2. Coat all sides of chicken and tofu with the sauce.
3. Marinate for 1 hour.
4. In a pan over medium heat, add 1 tablespoon oil.
5. Add carrot and cook for 2 minutes.
6. Add mushroom and cook for another 2 minutes.
7. Add bean sprouts, green onion and sweet pepper.
8. Cook for two to three minutes.
9. Stir in the chicken and heat through.

Nutritional Value:

- Calories 285
- Total Fat 9 g
- Saturated Fat 1 g
- Cholesterol 32 mg
- Sodium 331 mg
- Total Carbohydrate 30 g
- Dietary Fiber 4 g
- Total Sugars 4 g
- Protein 20 g
- Potassium 559 mg

Chicken & Peanut Stir-Fry

Preparation Time: 15 minutes
Cooking Time: 15 minutes
Servings: 4

Ingredients:

- 3 tablespoons lime juice
- ½ teaspoon lime zest
- 4 cloves garlic, minced
- 2 teaspoons chili bean sauce
- 1 tablespoon fish sauce
- 1 tablespoon water
- 2 tablespoons peanut butter
- 3 teaspoons oil, divided
- 1 lb. chicken breast, sliced into strips
- 1 red sweet pepper, sliced into strips
- 3 green onions, sliced thinly
- 2 cups broccoli, shredded
- 2 tablespoons peanuts, chopped

Method:
1. In a bowl, mix the lime juice, lime zest, garlic, chili bean sauce, fish sauce, water and peanut butter.
2. Mix well.
3. In a pan over medium high heat, add 2 teaspoons of oil.
4. Cook the chicken until golden on both sides.
5. Pour in the remaining oil.
6. Add the pepper and green onions.
7. Add the chicken, broccoli and sauce.
8. Cook for 2 minutes.
9. Top with peanuts before serving.

Nutritional Value:

- Calories 368
- Total Fat 11 g
- Saturated Fat 2 g
- Cholesterol 66 mg
- Sodium 556 mg
- Total Carbohydrate 34 g
- Dietary Fiber 3 g
- Total Sugars 4 g
- Protein 32 g
- Potassium 482 mg

Honey Mustard Chicken

Preparation Time: 15 minutes
Cooking Time: 12 minutes
Servings: 4

Ingredients:

- 2 tablespoons honey mustard
- 2 teaspoons olive oil
- Salt to taste
- 1 lb. chicken tenders
- 1 lb. baby carrots, steamed
- Chopped parsley

Method:

1. Preheat your oven to 450 degrees F.
2. Mix honey mustard, olive oil and salt.
3. Coat the chicken tenders with the mixture.
4. Place the chicken on a single layer on the baking pan.
5. Bake for 10 to 12 minutes.
6. Serve with steamed carrots and garnish with parsley.

Nutritional Value:

- Calories 366
- Total Fat 8 g
- Saturated Fat 2 g
- Cholesterol 63 mg
- Sodium 543 mg
- Total Carbohydrate 46 g
- Dietary Fiber 8 g
- Total Sugars 13 g
- Protein 33 g
- Potassium 377 mg

Lemon Garlic Turkey

Preparation Time: 1 hour and 10 minutes
Cooking Time: 5 minutes
Servings: 4

Ingredients:

- 4 turkey breasts fillet
- 2 cloves garlic, minced
- 1 tablespoon olive oil
- 3 tablespoons lemon juice
- 1 oz. Parmesan cheese, shredded
- Pepper to taste
- 1 tablespoon fresh sage, snipped
- 1 teaspoon lemon zest

Method:

1. Pound the turkey breast until flat.
2. In a bowl, mix the olive oil, garlic and lemon juice.
3. Add the turkey to the bowl.
4. Marinate for 1 hour.
5. Broil for 5 minutes until turkey is fully cooked.
6. Sprinkle cheese on top on the last minute of cooking.
7. In a bowl, mix the pepper, sage and lemon zest.
8. Sprinkle this mixture on top of the turkey before serving.

Nutritional Value:

- Calories 188
- Total Fat 7 g
- Saturated Fat 2 g
- Cholesterol 71 mg
- Sodium 173 mg
- Total Carbohydrate 2 g
- Dietary Fiber 0 g
- Total Sugars 0 g
- Protein 29 g
- Potassium 264 mg

Chicken & Spinach

Preparation Time: 15 minutes
Cooking Time: 13 minutes
Servings: 4

Ingredients:

- 2 tablespoons olive oil
- 1 lb. chicken breast fillet, sliced into small pieces
- Salt and pepper to taste
- 4 cloves garlic, minced
- 1 tablespoon lemon juice
- ½ cup dry white wine
- 1 teaspoon lemon zest
- 10 cups fresh spinach, chopped
- 4 tablespoons Parmesan cheese, grated

Method:

1. Pour oil in a pan over medium heat.
2. Season chicken with salt and pepper.
3. Cook in the pan for 7 minutes until golden on both sides.
4. Add the garlic and cook for 1 minute.
5. Stir in the lemon juice and wine.
6. Sprinkle lemon zest on top.
7. Simmer for 5 minutes.
8. Add the spinach and cook until wilted.
9. Serve with Parmesan cheese.

Nutritional Value:

- Calories 334
- Total Fat 12 g
- Saturated Fat 3 g
- Cholesterol 67 mg
- Sodium 499 mg
- Total Carbohydrate 25 g
- Dietary Fiber 2 g
- Total Sugars 1 g
- Protein 29 g
- Potassium 685 mg

Balsamic Chicken

Preparation Time: 15 minutes
Cooking Time: 5 hours
Servings: 6

Ingredients:

- 6 chicken breast halves, skin removed
- 1 onion, sliced into wedges
- 1 tablespoon tapioca (quick cooking), crushed
- Salt and pepper to taste
- 1 teaspoon dried thyme, crushed
- 1 teaspoon dried rosemary, crushed
- ¼ cup balsamic vinegar
- 2 tablespoons chicken broth
- 9 oz. frozen Italian green beans
- 1 red sweet pepper, sliced into strips

Method:

1. Put the chicken, onion and tapioca inside a slow cooker.
2. Season with the salt, pepper, thyme and rosemary.
3. Seal the pot and cook on low setting for 4 hours and 30 minutes.
4. Add the sweet pepper and green beans.
5. Cook for 30 more minutes.
6. Pour sauce over the chicken and vegetables before serving.

Nutritional Value:

- Calories 234
- Total Fat 2 g
- Saturated Fat 1 g
- Cholesterol 100 mg
- Sodium 308 mg
- Total Carbohydrate 10 g
- Dietary Fiber 2 g
- Total Sugars 5 g
- Protein 41 g
- Potassium 501 mg

Greek Chicken Lettuce Wraps

Preparation Time: 1 hour and 15 minutes
Cooking Time: 8 minutes
Servings: 4

Ingredients:

- 2 tablespoons freshly squeezed lemon juice
- 1 teaspoon lemon zest
- 5 teaspoons olive oil, divided
- 3 teaspoons garlic, minced and divided
- 1 teaspoon dried oregano
- ¼ teaspoon red pepper, crushed
- 1 lb. chicken tenders
- 1 cucumber, sliced in half and grated
- Salt and pepper to taste
- ¾ cup non-fat Greek yogurt
- 2 teaspoons fresh mint, chopped
- 2 teaspoons fresh dill, chopped
- 4 lettuce leaves
- ½ cup red onion, sliced
- 1 cup tomatoes, chopped

Method:

1. In a bowl, mix the lemon juice, lemon zest, half of oil, half of garlic, and red pepper.
2. Coat the chicken with the marinade.
3. Marinate it for 1 hour.
4. Toss grated cucumber in salt.
5. Squeeze to release liquid.
6. Add the yogurt, dill, salt, pepper, remaining garlic and remaining oil.
7. Grill the chicken for 4 minutes per side.
8. Shred the chicken and put on top of the lettuce leaves.
9. Top with the yogurt mixture, onion and tomatoes.
10. Wrap the lettuce leaves and secure with a toothpick.

Nutritional Value:

- Calories 353
- Total Fat 9 g
- Saturated Fat 1 g
- Cholesterol 58 mg
- Sodium 559 mg
- Total Carbohydrate 33 g
- Dietary Fiber 6 g
- Total Sugars 6 g
- Protein 37 g
- Potassium 459 mg

Lemon Chicken with Kale

Preparation Time: 10 minutes
Cooking Time: 19 minutes
Servings: 4

Ingredients:

- 1 tablespoon olive oil
- 1 lb. chicken thighs, trimmed
- Salt and pepper to taste
- ½ cup low-sodium chicken stock
- 1 lemon, sliced
- 1 tablespoon fresh tarragon, chopped
- 4 cloves garlic, minced
- 6 cups baby kale

Method:

1. Pour olive oil in a pan over medium heat.
2. Season chicken with salt and pepper.
3. Cook until golden brown on both sides.
4. Pour in the stock.
5. Add the lemon, tarragon and garlic.
6. Simmer for 15 minutes.
7. Add the kale and cook for 4 minutes.

Nutritional Value:

- Calories 374
- Total Fat 19 g
- Saturated Fat 4 g
- Cholesterol 76 mg
- Sodium 378 mg
- Total Carbohydrate 26 g
- Dietary Fiber 3 g
- Total Sugars 2 g
- Protein 25 g
- Potassium 677 mg

Chapter 9: Vegetarian Recipes

Kale & Tofu Salad

Preparation Time: 20 minutes
Cooking Time: 15 minutes
Servings: 4

Ingredients:

- 1 block tofu, sliced into cubes
- ¼ cup Worcestershire sauce
- ¼ cup freshly squeezed lemon juice
- 1 teaspoon onion powder
- 1 teaspoon garlic powder
- 3 teaspoons olive oil
- 8 cups kale, chopped
- ¼ cup nutritional yeast
- ¼ cup pumpkin seeds, toasted
- ½ cup Caesar dressing
- 1 avocado, sliced

Method:

1. Dry the tofu with paper towel.
2. In a bowl, mix the Worcestershire sauce, lemon juice, onion powder and garlic powder.
3. Coat the tofu with this mixture.
4. Let it stand for 15 minutes.
5. Discard the marinade.
6. Pour the oil in a pan over medium heat.
7. Cook the tofu until golden brown on all sides.
8. Drain the oil and set aside.
9. In a bowl, toss the kale in nutritional yeast.
10. Divide into containers.
11. Top each container with croutons and pumpkin seeds.
12. Pour dressing on top and serve with avocado slices.

Nutritional Value:

- Calories 400
- Total Fat 28 g
- Saturated Fat 4 g
- Cholesterol 6 mg
- Sodium 423 mg
- Total Carbohydrate 19 g
- Dietary Fiber 9 g
- Total Sugars 2 g
- Protein 20 g
- Potassium 670 mg

Boiled Potatoes with Tomato Salsa

Preparation Time: 15 minutes
Cooking Time: 15 minutes
Servings: 8

Ingredients:

- 6 potatoes, sliced into wedges
- 1 clove garlic, minced
- 3 large tomatoes, diced
- 2 tablespoons white onion, chopped
- 2 teaspoons fresh marjoram, chopped
- Salt and pepper to taste

Method:

1. Boil the potatoes until soft enough to poke with a fork.
2. Combine the rest of the ingredients in a bowl.
3. Serve potatoes with salsa.

Nutritional Value:

- Calories 200
- Total Fat 10 g
- Saturated Fat 1 g
- Cholesterol 25 mg
- Sodium 81 mg
- Total Carbohydrate 10 g
- Dietary Fiber 5 g
- Total Sugars 1 g
- Protein 25 g
- Potassium 560 mg

Braised Summer Squash

Preparation Time: 15 minutes
Cooking Time: 20 minutes
Servings: 6

Ingredients:

- ¼ cup olive oil
- 4 cloves garlic, crushed
- ¼ teaspoon red pepper, crushed
- ½ teaspoon anchovy paste
- 1 lb. zucchini, sliced into small cubes
- 1 lb. summer squash, sliced into small cubes
- Salt to taste
- 1 tablespoon fresh oregano, chopped

Method:

1. Pour the oil in a pan over medium heat.
2. Add the garlic, red pepper and anchovy paste.
3. Cook for 3 minutes.
4. Add the zucchini and squash.
5. Cook for 15 minutes.
6. Season with salt and oregano.

Nutritional Value:

- Calories 140
- Total Fat 13 g
- Saturated Fat 2 g
- Cholesterol 0 mg
- Sodium 202 mg
- Total Carbohydrate 6 g
- Dietary Fiber 2 g
- Total Sugars 3 g
- Protein 2 g
- Potassium 408 mg

Grilled Potatoes in a Packet

Preparation Time: 10 minutes
Cooking Time: 35 minutes
Servings: 6

Ingredients:

- 1 ½ lb. potatoes, sliced into wedges
- 2 cloves garlic, sliced
- 2 tablespoons olive oil
- Salt and pepper to taste
- 1 teaspoon dried rosemary

Method:

1. Preheat your grill.
2. Create a packet using foil.
3. Drizzle oil over the potatoes and season with salt, pepper and rosemary.
4. Place potatoes inside the packet.
5. Fold and seal.
6. Grill for 15 minutes.
7. Turn to the other side.
8. Grill for 20 minutes.
9. Remove from the grill and open cautiously.
10. Serve while warm.

Nutritional Value:

- Calories 148
- Total Fat 6 g
- Saturated Fat 1 g
- Cholesterol 0 mg
- Sodium 141 mg
- Total Carbohydrate 22 g
- Dietary Fiber 2 g
- Total Sugars 2 g
- Protein 3 g
- Potassium 626 mg

Mixed Greens Salad

Preparation Time: 15 minutes
Cooking Time: 0 minutes
Servings: 6

Ingredients:

- 6 cups mixed salad greens
- 1 cup cucumber, chopped
- ½ cup carrot, shredded
- ¼ cup bell pepper, sliced into strips
- ¼ cup cherry tomatoes, sliced in half
- 6 tablespoons white onion, chopped
- 6 tablespoons balsamic vinaigrette dressing

Method:

1. Toss all the ingredients in a large salad bowl.
2. Drizzle dressing on top or serve on the side.

Nutritional Value:

- Calories 23
- Total Fat 1 g
- Saturated Fat 0 g
- Cholesterol 0 mg
- Sodium 138 mg
- Total Carbohydrate 4 g
- Dietary Fiber 1 g
- Total Sugars 1 g
- Protein 1 g
- Potassium 142 mg

Roasted Carrots

Preparation Time: 15 minutes
Cooking Time: 20 minutes
Servings: 4

Ingredients:

- 2 tablespoons olive oil, divided
- 2 tablespoons balsamic vinegar
- 1 tablespoon pure maple syrup
- 1 lb. carrots, sliced into small pieces
- Salt to taste
- 2 tablespoons hazelnuts, chopped

Method:

1. Preheat your oven to 400 degrees F.
2. Combine 1 tablespoon oil with vinegar and maple syrup.
3. Set aside the mixture.
4. In another bowl, toss the carrots in remaining oil and season with salt.
5. Arrange on a single layer in a baking pan.
6. Roast for 15 minutes.
7. Pour the reserved mixture over the carrots and mix.
8. Roast for additional 5 minutes.
9. Sprinkle hazelnuts on top before serving.

Nutritional Value:

- Calories 130
- Total Fat 7 g
- Saturated Fat 1g
- Cholesterol 0 mg
- Sodium 226 mg
- Total Carbohydrate 16 g
- Dietary Fiber 3 g
- Total Sugars 10 g
- Protein 1 g
- Potassium 382 mg

Porcini Mushrooms & Eggplant

Preparation Time: 20 minutes
Cooking Time: 30 minutes
Servings: 6

Ingredients:

- 1 lb. eggplant, cubed
- 2 tablespoons olive oil
- Salt and pepper to taste
- ½ oz. dried porcini mushrooms
- 1 cup boiling water
- ⅓ cup balsamic vinegar
- 1 teaspoon fresh thyme, chopped
- ½ cup cherry tomatoes, sliced in half
- 1 tablespoon fresh basil, chopped

Method:

1. Preheat your oven to 425 degrees F.
2. Arrange the eggplant cubes on a baking pan.
3. Drizzle oil on top and season with salt and pepper.
4. Roast for 15 minutes.
5. While waiting, soak mushrooms in hot water.
6. Let it sit for 15 minutes.
7. Drain water, and then chop.
8. Pour the vinegar in a saucepan over medium heat.
9. Bring to a boil and then reduce heat to simmer for 5 minutes.
10. Add the mushrooms and fresh thyme.
11. Drizzle balsamic mixture on top of the eggplants and serve with the tomatoes with basil.

Nutritional Value:

- Calories 77
- Total Fat 5 g
- Saturated Fat 1 g
- Cholesterol 0 mg
- Sodium 103 mg
- Total Carbohydrate 8 g
- Dietary Fiber 3 g
- Total Sugars 4 g
- Protein 1 g
- Potassium 232 mg

Kale with Miso & Ginger

Preparation Time: 10 minutes
Cooking Time: 10 minutes
Servings: 6

Ingredients:

- 8 oz. fresh kale, sliced into strips
- 1 clove garlic, minced
- 1 tablespoon lime juice
- ½ teaspoon lime zest
- 2 tablespoons oil
- 2 tablespoons rice vinegar
- 1 teaspoon fresh ginger, grated
- 2 teaspoons miso
- 2 tablespoons dry roasted cashews, chopped

Method:

1. Steam kale on a steamer basket in a pot with water.
2. Transfer kale to a bowl.
3. Mix the rest of the ingredients except cashews in another bowl.
4. Toss kale in the mixture.
5. Top with chopped cashews before serving.

Nutritional Value:

- Calories 86
- Total Fat 5 g
- Saturated Fat 0 g
- Cholesterol 0 mg
- Sodium 104 mg
- Total Carbohydrate 9 g
- Dietary Fiber 2 g
- Total Sugars 2 g
- Protein 3 g
- Potassium 352 mg

Grilled Zucchini with Tomato Relish

Preparation Time: 10 minutes
Cooking Time: 10 minutes
Servings: 4

Ingredients:

- 1 lb. zucchini, sliced in half
- 1 tablespoon olive oil
- Salt and pepper to taste
- 1 teaspoon red wine vinegar
- 1 tablespoon mint, chopped
- 1 cup tomatoes, chopped

Method:

1. Preheat your grill.
2. Brush both sides of zucchini with oil and season with salt and pepper.
3. Grill for 3 to 4 minutes per side.
4. In a bowl, mix the rest of the ingredients with the remaining oil.
5. Season with salt and pepper.
6. Spread tomato relish on top of the grilled zucchini before serving.

Nutritional Value:

- Calories 71
- Total Fat 5 g
- Saturated Fat 1 g
- Cholesterol 0 mg
- Sodium 157 mg
- Total Carbohydrate 6 g
- Dietary Fiber 2 g
- Total Sugars 4 g
- Protein 2 g
- Potassium 413 mg

Cucumber Salad with Pesto

Preparation Time: 15 minutes
Cooking Time: 0 minute
Servings: 4

Ingredients:

- 1 cup fresh basil leaves, chopped
- 2 cloves garlic
- 2 tablespoons walnuts
- 1 teaspoon Parmesan cheese
- 1 tablespoon olive oil
- 2 cucumbers, sliced into rounds
- Salt and pepper to taste

Method:

1. Put the basil, garlic, walnuts, Parmesan cheese and olive oil in a food processor.
2. Pulse until smooth.
3. Season the cucumbers with salt and pepper.
4. Spread pesto on top of each cucumber round.

Nutritional Value:

- Calories 80
- Total Fat 6g
- Saturated Fat 0.7g
- Cholesterol 0mg
- Sodium 4mg
- Total Carbohydrate 6.5g
- Dietary Fiber 1.2g
- Total Sugars 2.6g
- Protein 2.2g
- Potassium 266mg

Chapter 10: Side Recipes

Fried Okra

Preparation Time: 15 minutes
Cooking Time: 15 minutes
Servings: 4

Ingredients:

- 2 teaspoons Cajun seasoning, divided
- 1 cup buttermilk
- 8 oz. okra
- ½ cup white whole-wheat flour
- ½ cup cornstarch
- ⅓ cup oil
- Salt to taste

Method:

1. Mix half of the Cajun seasoning and buttermilk in a bowl.
2. Add the okra.
3. Mix well.
4. Let sit for 10 minutes.
5. In another bowl, blend the remaining Cajun seasoning, flour and cornstarch.
6. Drain the okra.
7. Dip each okra in the flour mixture.
8. Pour the oil in a pan over medium high heat.
9. Cook the okra until golden on all sides.
10. Season with salt before serving.

Nutritional Value:

- Calories 106
- Total Fat 5 g
- Saturated Fat 0 g
- Cholesterol 0 mg
- Sodium 75 mg
- Total Carbohydrate 14 g
- Dietary Fiber 2 g
- Total Sugars 1 g
- Protein 2 g
- Potassium 195 mg

Grilled Sweet Potatoes

Preparation Time: 15 minutes
Cooking Time: 25 minutes
Servings: 4

Ingredients:

- 2 teaspoons orange zest
- 2 tablespoons fresh mint, minted
- 1 teaspoon raw sugar
- Salt and pepper to taste
- 1 lb. sweet potatoes, sliced into wedges
- 1 tablespoon olive oil
- 1 tablespoon butter (unsalted)

Method:

1. Preheat your grill.
2. Mix the orange zest, mint, sugar and salt in a bowl.
3. Set aside.
4. Toss the sweet potatoes in olive oil and season with salt and pepper.
5. Grill for 25 minutes, turning once or twice.
6. Let the butter melt on top of the sweet potatoes.
7. Serve with the reserved mixture.

Nutritional Value:

- Calories 131
- Total Fat 7 g
- Saturated Fat 2 g
- Cholesterol 8 mg
- Sodium 98 mg
- Total Carbohydrate 17 g
- Dietary Fiber 3 g
- Total Sugars 6 g
- Protein 1 g
- Potassium 221 mg

Zucchini Fries

Preparation Time: 15 minutes
Cooking Time: 10 minutes
Servings: 6

Ingredients:

- Cooking spray
- ½ cup whole-wheat flour, divided
- 1 ¼ lb. zucchini, sliced into strips
- 2 egg whites, beaten
- ¼ cup low-fat buttermilk
- ½ cup fine dry whole-wheat breadcrumbs
- Garlic salt and pepper to taste

Method:

1. Preheat your oven to 450 degrees F.
2. Spray oil on a baking sheet.
3. Put half of the flour in a resealable plastic bag.
4. Add the zucchini strips to the bag.
5. Seal and then shake to coat.
6. In a shallow dish, mix the egg whites and buttermilk.
7. In a separate bowl, mix the remaining flour, breadcrumbs and garlic salt.
8. Dip each zucchini strip in the egg mixture and then dredge with the seasoned flour mixture.
9. Place on a baking sheet.
10. Bake in the oven for 7 minutes or until the zucchini fries are golden and crispy.

Nutritional Value:

- Calories 94
- Total Fat 1 g
- Saturated Fat 0 g
- Cholesterol 1 mg
- Sodium 123 mg
- Total Carbohydrate 15 g
- Dietary Fiber 2 g
- Total Sugars 5 g
- Protein 6 g
- Potassium 326 mg

French Green Beans

Preparation Time: 10 minutes
Cooking Time: 5 minutes
Servings: 4

Ingredients:

- Water
- 2 cups green beans, rinsed, drained and trimmed
- 1 tablespoon shallot, minced
- 2 teaspoons olive oil
- 2 teaspoons fresh thyme, chopped
- Salt and pepper to taste

Method:

1. Put a steamer basket in a large pan.
2. Add water to the bottom of the pan.
3. Bring it to a boil.
4. Put the beans on top of the basket and cover.
5. Reduce heat and steam for 2 minutes.
6. Drain and then rinse with cold water.
7. In a bowl, mix the rest of the ingredients.
8. Toss the beans in the mixture.

Nutritional Value:

- Calories 38
- Total Fat 2 g
- Saturated Fat 0 g
- Cholesterol 0 mg
- Sodium 149 mg
- Total Carbohydrate 4 g
- Dietary Fiber 2 g
- Total Sugars 1 g
- Protein 1 g
- Potassium 117 mg

Roasted Summer Squash

Preparation Time: 15 minutes
Cooking Time: 15 minutes
Servings: 4

Ingredients:

- Cooking spray
- 2 summer squash, sliced into strips
- 1 ½ teaspoons olive oil
- Garlic salt and pepper to taste
- Parmesan cheese

Method:

1. Preheat your oven to 425 degrees F.
2. Line a baking sheet with foil
3. Spray oil on the foil.
4. Toss the squash strips in the olive oil and season with salt and pepper.
5. Arrange on a single layer on the pan.
6. Roast for 15 minutes.
7. Sprinkle with Parmesan cheese before serving.

Nutritional Value:

- Calories 33
- Total Fat 2 g
- Saturated Fat 0 g
- Cholesterol 0 mg
- Sodium 132 mg
- Total Carbohydrate 3 g
- Dietary Fiber 1 g
- Total Sugars 3 g
- Protein 1 g
- Potassium 282 mg

Veggie Mash

Preparation Time: 15 minutes
Cooking Time: 35 minutes
Servings: 4

Ingredients:

- 1 onion, sliced into wedges
- 2 cloves garlic, sliced in half
- 2 carrots, sliced into wedges
- 1 sweet potato, sliced into strips
- 4 teaspoons olive oil
- Salt and pepper to taste
- 1 teaspoon fresh ginger, grated
- 3 tablespoons nonfat milk

Method:

1. Preheat your oven to 425 degrees F.
2. Put the onion, garlic, carrots and sweet potato in a baking pan.
3. Drizzle with oil and toss to coat evenly.
4. Cover with foil and roast for 25 minutes.
5. Take the vegetables out of the foil and roast for another 10 minutes.
6. Transfer to a food processor.
7. Add the salt, pepper and ginger.
8. Pulse until smooth.
9. Gradually add milk until desired consistency is achieved.

Nutritional Value:

- Calories 114
- Total Fat 5 g
- Saturated Fat 1 g
- Cholesterol 0mg
- Sodium 202 mg
- Total Carbohydrate 17 g
- Dietary Fiber 3 g
- Total Sugars 5 g
- Protein 2 g
- Potassium 336 mg

Mushroom Medley

Preparation Time: 15 minutes
Cooking Time: 25 minutes
Servings: 6

Ingredients:

- 1 lb. assorted fresh mushrooms, sliced
- 6 cloves garlic, sliced thinly
- 2 teaspoons balsamic vinegar
- 2 tablespoons olive oil
- 2 teaspoons Worcestershire sauce
- 1 teaspoon dried oregano, crushed
- Salt and pepper to taste
- 2 tablespoons fresh Italian parsley, chopped

Method:

1. Preheat your oven to 400 degrees F.
2. Put the mushrooms on a baking sheet.
3. Stir in the garlic slices.
4. In a bowl, mix the vinegar, olive oil and Worcestershire sauce.
5. Toss the mushroom and garlic in this mixture.
6. Season with oregano, salt and pepper.
7. Roast for 25 minutes.
8. Sprinkle parsley on top before serving.

Nutritional Value:

- Calories 65
- Total Fat 5 g
- Saturated Fat 1 g
- Cholesterol 0 mg
- Sodium 124 mg
- Total Carbohydrate 4 g
- Dietary Fiber 1 g
- Total Sugars 1 g
- Protein 25 g
- Potassium 459 mg

Mustard Potatoes

Preparation Time: 20 minutes
Cooking Time: 45 minutes
Servings: 12

Ingredients:

- 4 lb. potatoes, sliced into wedges
- Cooking spray
- 3 tablespoons olive oil
- Salt and pepper to taste
- ½ teaspoon ground turmeric
- 2 teaspoons dry mustard
- 1 tablespoon coriander seeds, crushed
- 1 tablespoon mustard seeds, crushed
- ¼ cup fresh Italian parsley, chopped

Method:

1. Preheat your oven to 450 degrees F.
2. Coat a baking pan with oil.
3. Toss potatoes in olive oil, salt, pepper, turmeric and dry mustard.
4. Arrange on a single layer on a pan.
5. Roast for 15 minutes.
6. Add the coriander and mustard seeds.
7. Roast for another 10 minutes.
8. Garnish with parsley before serving.

Nutritional Value:

- Calories 155
- Total Fat 4 g
- Saturated Fat 1 g
- Cholesterol 0 mg
- Sodium 156 mg
- Total Carbohydrate 27 g
- Dietary Fiber 4 g
- Total Sugars 1 g
- Protein 3 g
- Potassium 665 mg

Chapter 11: Fish and Seafood Recipes

Grilled Salmon with Ginger Sauce

Preparation Time: 15 minutes
Cooking Time: 8 minutes
Servings: 4

Ingredients:

- 1 tablespoon toasted sesame oil
- 1 tablespoon fresh cilantro, chopped
- 1 tablespoon lime juice
- 1 teaspoon fish sauce
- 1 clove garlic, mashed
- 1 teaspoon fresh ginger, grated
- 1 teaspoon jalapeño pepper, minced
- 4 salmon fillets
- 1 tablespoon olive oil
- Salt and pepper to taste

Method:

1. In a bowl, mix the sesame oil, cilantro, lime juice, fish sauce, garlic, ginger and jalapeño pepper.
2. Preheat your grill.
3. Brush oil on salmon.
4. Season both sides with salt and pepper.
5. Grill salmon for 6 to 8 minutes, turning once or twice.
6. Take 1 tablespoon from the oil mixture.
7. Brush this on the salmon while grilling.
8. Serve grilled salmon with the remaining sauce.

Nutritional Value:

- Calories 204
- Total Fat 11 g
- Saturated Fat 2 g
- Cholesterol 53 mg
- Sodium 320 mg
- Total Carbohydrate 2 g
- Dietary Fiber 0 g
- Total Sugars 2 g
- Protein 23 g
- Potassium 437 mg

Almond Crusted Baked Chili Mahi Mahi

Preparation Time: 20 minutes
Cooking Time: 15 minutes
Servings: 4

Ingredients:

- 4 mahi mahi fillets
- 1 lime
- 2 teaspoons olive oil
- Salt and pepper to taste
- ½ cup almonds
- ¼ teaspoon paprika
- ¼ teaspoon onion powder
- ¾ teaspoon chili powder
- ½ cup red bell pepper, chopped
- ¼ cup onion, chopped
- ¼ cup fresh cilantro, chopped

Method:

1. Preheat your oven to 325 degrees F.
2. Line your baking pan with parchment paper.
3. Squeeze juice from the lime.
4. Grate zest from the peel.
5. Put juice and zest in a bowl.
6. Add the oil, salt and pepper.
7. In another bowl, add the almonds, paprika, onion powder and chili powder.
8. Put the almond mixture in a food processor.
9. Pulse until powdery.
10. Dip each fillet in the oil mixture.
11. Dredge with the almond and chili mixture.
12. Arrange on a single layer in the oven.
13. Bake for 12 to 15 minutes or until fully cooked.
14. Serve with red bell pepper, onion and cilantro.

Nutritional Value:

- Calories 322
- Total Fat 12 g
- Saturated Fat 2 g
- Cholesterol 83 mg
- Sodium 328 mg
- Total Carbohydrate 28 g
- Dietary Fiber 4 g
- Total Sugars 10 g
- Protein 28 g
- Potassium 829 mg

Swordfish with Tomato Salsa

Preparation Time: 20 minutes
Cooking Time: 12 minutes
Servings: 4

Ingredients:

- 1 cup tomato, chopped
- ¼ cup tomatillo, chopped
- 2 tablespoons fresh cilantro, chopped
- ¼ cup avocado, chopped
- 1 clove garlic, minced
- 1 jalapeño pepper, chopped
- 1 tablespoon lime juice
- Salt and pepper to taste
- 4 swordfish steaks
- 1 clove garlic, sliced in half
- 2 tablespoons lemon juice
- ½ teaspoon ground cumin

Method:

1. Preheat your grill.
2. In a bowl, mix the tomato, tomatillo, cilantro, avocado, garlic, jalapeño, lime juice, salt and pepper.
3. Cover the bowl with foil and put in the refrigerator.
4. Rub each swordfish steak with sliced garlic.
5. Drizzle lemon juice on both sides.
6. Season with salt, pepper and cumin.
7. Grill for 12 minutes or until the fish is fully cooked.
8. Serve with salsa.

Nutritional Value:

- Calories 190
- Total Fat 8 g
- Saturated Fat 2 g
- Cholesterol 43 mg
- Sodium 254 mg
- Total Carbohydrate 6 g
- Dietary Fiber 3 g
- Total Sugars 1 g
- Protein 24 g
- Potassium 453 mg

Salmon & Asparagus

Preparation Time: 15 minutes
Cooking Time: 10 minutes
Servings: 2

Ingredients:

- 2 salmon fillets
- 8 spears asparagus, trimmed
- 2 tablespoons balsamic vinegar
- 1 teaspoon olive oil
- 1 teaspoon dried dill
- Salt and pepper to taste

Method:

1. Preheat your oven to 325 degrees F.
2. Dry salmon with paper towels.
3. Arrange the asparagus around the salmon fillets on a baking pan.
4. In a bowl, mix the rest of the ingredients.
5. Pour mixture over the salmon and vegetables.
6. Bake in the oven for 10 minutes or until the fish is fully cooked.

Nutritional Value:

- Calories 328
- Total Fat 15 g
- Saturated Fat 3 g
- Cholesterol 67 mg
- Sodium 365 mg
- Total Carbohydrate 6 g
- Dietary Fiber 4 g
- Total Sugars 5 g
- Protein 28 g
- Potassium 258 mg

Halibut with Spicy Apricot Sauce

Preparation Time: 15 minutes
Cooking Time: 17 minutes
Servings: 4

Ingredients:

- 4 fresh apricots, pitted
- ⅓ cup apricot preserves
- ½ cup apricot nectar
- ½ teaspoon dried oregano
- 3 tablespoons scallion, sliced
- 1 teaspoon hot pepper sauce
- Salt to taste
- 4 halibut steaks
- 1 tablespoon olive oil

Method:

1. Put the apricots, preserves, nectar, oregano, scallion, hot pepper sauce and salt in a saucepan.
2. Bring to a boil and then simmer for 8 minutes.
3. Set aside.
4. Brush the halibut steaks with olive oil.
5. Grill for 7 to 9 minutes or until fish is flaky.
6. Brush one tablespoon of the sauce on both sides of the fish.
7. Serve with the reserved sauce.

Nutritional Value:

- Calories 304
- Total Fat 8 g
- Saturated Fat 1 g
- Cholesterol 73 mg
- Sodium 260 mg
- Total Carbohydrate 27 g
- Dietary Fiber 2 g
- Total Sugars 16 g
- Protein 29 g
- Potassium 637 mg

Popcorn Shrimp

Preparation Time: 15 minutes
Cooking Time: 8 minutes
Servings: 4

Ingredients:

- Cooking spray
- ½ cup all-purpose flour
- 2 eggs, beaten
- 2 tablespoons water
- 1 ½ cups panko breadcrumbs
- 1 tablespoon garlic powder
- 1 tablespoon ground cumin
- 1 lb. shrimp, peeled and deveined
- ½ cup ketchup
- 2 tablespoons fresh cilantro, chopped
- 2 tablespoons lime juice
- Salt to taste

Method:

1. Coat the air fryer basket with cooking spray
2. Put the flour in a dish.
3. In the second dish, beat the eggs and water.
4. In the third dish, mix the breadcrumbs, garlic powder and cumin.
5. Dip each shrimp in each of the three dishes, first in the dish with flour, then the egg and then breadcrumb mixture.
6. Place the shrimp in the air fryer basket.
7. Cook at 360 degrees F for 8 minutes, flipping once halfway through.
8. Combine the rest of the ingredients as dipping sauce for the shrimp.

Nutritional Value:

- Calories 297
- Total Fat 4 g
- Saturated Fat 1 g
- Cholesterol 276 mg
- Sodium 291 mg
- Total Carbohydrate 35 g
- Dietary Fiber 1 g
- Total Sugars 9 g
- Protein 29 g
- Potassium 390 mg

Shrimp Lemon Kebab

Preparation Time: 10 minutes
Cooking Time: 5 minutes
Servings: 4

Ingredients:

- 1 ½ lb. shrimp, peeled and deveined but with tails intact
- ⅓ cup olive oil
- ¼ cup lemon juice
- 2 teaspoons lemon zest
- 1 tablespoon fresh parsley, chopped
- 8 cherry tomatoes, quartered
- 2 scallions, sliced

Method:

1. Mix the olive oil, lemon juice, lemon zest and parsley in a bowl.
2. Marinate the shrimp in this mixture for 15 minutes.
3. Thread each shrimp into the skewers.
4. Grill for 4 to 5 minutes, turning once halfway through.
5. Serve with tomatoes and scallions.

Nutritional Value:

- Calories 271
- Total Fat 12 g
- Saturated Fat 2 g
- Cholesterol 259 mg
- Sodium 255 mg
- Total Carbohydrate 4 g
- Dietary Fiber 1 g
- Total Sugars 1 g
- Protein 25 g
- Potassium 429 mg

Grilled Herbed Salmon with Raspberry Sauce & Cucumber Dill Dip

Preparation Time: 15 minutes
Cooking Time: 30 minutes
Servings: 4

Ingredients:

- 3 salmon fillets
- 1 tablespoon olive oil
- Salt and pepper to taste
- 1 teaspoon fresh sage, chopped
- 1 tablespoon fresh parsley, chopped
- 2 tablespoons apple juice
- 1 cup raspberries
- 1 teaspoon Worcestershire sauce
- 1 cup cucumber, chopped
- 2 tablespoons light mayonnaise
- ½ teaspoon dried dill

Method:

1. Coat the salmon fillets with oil.
2. Season with salt, pepper, sage and parsley.
3. Cover the salmon with foil.
4. Grill for 20 minutes or until fish is flaky.
5. While waiting, mix the apple juice, raspberries and Worcestershire sauce.
6. Pour the mixture into a saucepan over medium heat.
7. Bring to a boil and then simmer for 8 minutes.
8. In another bowl, mix the rest of the ingredients.
9. Serve salmon with raspberry sauce and cucumber dip.

Nutritional Value:

- Calories 256
- Total Fat 15 g
- Saturated Fat 3 g
- Cholesterol 68 mg
- Sodium 176 mg
- Total Carbohydrate 6 g
- Dietary Fiber 1 g
- Total Sugars 5 g
- Protein 23 g
- Potassium 359 mg

Tarragon Scallops

Preparation Time: 10 minutes
Cooking Time: 15 minutes
Servings: 4

Ingredients:

- 1 cup water
- 1 lb. asparagus spears, trimmed
- 2 lemons
- 1 ¼ lb. scallops
- Salt and pepper to taste
- 1 tablespoon olive oil
- 1 tablespoon fresh tarragon, chopped

Method:

1. Pour water into a pot.
2. Bring to a boil.
3. Add asparagus spears.
4. Cover and cook for 5 minutes.
5. Drain and transfer to a plate.
6. Slice one lemon into wedges.
7. Squeeze juice and shred zest from the remaining lemon.
8. Season the scallops with salt and pepper.
9. Put a pan over medium heat.
10. Add oil to the pan.
11. Cook the scallops until golden brown.
12. Transfer to the same plate, putting scallops beside the asparagus.
13. Add lemon zest, juice and tarragon to the pan.
14. Cook for 1 minute.
15. Drizzle tarragon sauce over the scallops and asparagus.

Nutritional Value:

- Calories 253
- Total Fat 12 g
- Saturated Fat 2 g
- Cholesterol 47 mg
- Sodium 436 mg
- Total Carbohydrate 14 g
- Dietary Fiber 5 g
- Total Sugars 3 g
- Protein 27 g
- Potassium 773 mg

Garlic Shrimp & Spinach

Preparation Time: 10 minutes
Cooking Time: 10 minutes
Servings: 4

Ingredients:

- 3 tablespoons olive oil, divided
- 6 clove garlic, sliced and divided
- 1 lb. spinach
- Salt to taste
- 1 tablespoons lemon juice
- 1 lb. shrimp, peeled and deveined
- ¼ teaspoon red pepper, crushed
- 1 tablespoon parsley, chopped
- 1 teaspoon lemon zest

Method:

1. Pour 1 tablespoon olive oil in a pot over medium heat.
2. Cook the garlic for 1 minute.
3. Add the spinach and season with salt.
4. Cook for 3 minutes.
5. Stir in lemon juice.
6. Transfer to a bowl.
7. Pour the remaining oil.
8. Add the shrimp.
9. Season with salt and add red pepper.
10. Cook for 5 minutes.
11. Sprinkle parsley and lemon zest over the shrimp before serving.

Nutritional Value:

- Calories 226
- Total Fat 12 g
- Saturated Fat 2 g
- Cholesterol 183 mg
- Sodium 444 mg
- Total Carbohydrate 6 g
- Dietary Fiber 3 g
- Total Sugars 1 g
- Protein 26 g
- Potassium 963 mg

Chapter 12: Dessert Recipes

Chocolate & Raspberry Ice Cream

Preparation Time: 12 hours and 20 minutes
Cooking Time: 0 minutes
Servings: 8

Ingredients:

- ¼ cup almond milk
- 2 egg yolks
- 2 tablespoons cornstarch
- ¼ cup honey
- ¼ teaspoon almond extract
- ⅛ teaspoon salt
- 1 cup fresh raspberries
- 2 oz. dark chocolate, chopped
- ¼ cup almonds, slivered and toasted

Method:

1. Mix almond milk, egg yolks, cornstarch and honey in a bowl.
2. Pour into a saucepan over medium heat.
3. Cook for 8 minutes.
4. Strain through a sieve.
5. Stir in salt and almond extract.
6. Chill for 8 hours.
7. Put into an ice cream maker.
8. Follow manufacturer's directions.
9. Stir in the rest of the ingredients.
10. Freeze for 4 hours.

Nutritional Value:

- Calories 142
- Total Fat 7 g
- Saturated Fat 2 g
- Cholesterol 70 mg
- Sodium 87 mg
- Total Carbohydrate 18 g
- Dietary Fiber 2 g
- Total Sugars 13 g
- Protein 3 g
- Potassium 150 mg

Mocha Pops

Preparation Time: 4 minutes
Cooking Time: 0 minutes
Servings: 15

Ingredients:

- 3 cups brewed coffee
- ½ cup low calorie chocolate flavored syrup
- ¾ cup low fat half and half

Method:

1. Mix the ingredients in a bowl.
2. Pour into popsicle molds.
3. Freeze for 4 hours.

Nutritional Value:

- Calories 21
- Total Fat 0 g
- Saturated Fat 0 g
- Cholesterol 1 mg
- Sodium 28 mg
- Total Carbohydrate 4 g
- Dietary Fiber 0 g
- Total Sugars 3 g
- Protein 0 g
- Potassium 450 mg

Choco Banana Bites

Preparation Time: 2 hours and 5 minutes
Cooking Time: 5 minutes
Servings: 4

Ingredients:

- 2 bananas, sliced into rounds
- ¼ cup dark chocolate cubes

Method:

1. Melt chocolate in the microwave or in a saucepan over medium heat.
2. Coat each banana slice with melted chocolate.
3. Place on a metal pan.
4. Freeze for 2 hours.

Nutritional Value:

- Calories 102
- Total Fat 3 g
- Saturated Fat 2 g
- Cholesterol 0 mg
- Sodium 4 mg
- Total Carbohydrate 20 g
- Dietary Fiber 2 g
- Total Sugars 13 g
- Protein 1 g
- Potassium 211 mg

Blueberries with Yogurt

Preparation Time: 5 minutes
Cooking Time: 0 minute
Serving: 1

Ingredients:

- 1 cup nonfat Greek yogurt
- ¼ cup blueberries
- ¼ cup almonds

Method:

1. Add yogurt and blueberries in a food processor.
2. Pulse until smooth.
3. Top with almonds before serving.

Nutritional Value:

- Calories 154
- Total Fat 1 g
- Saturated Fat 0 g
- Cholesterol 11 mg
- Sodium 81 mg
- Total Carbohydrate 13 g
- Dietary Fiber 1 g
- Total Sugars 11 g
- Protein 23 g
- Potassium 346 mg

Fruit Kebab

Preparation Time: 30 minutes
Cooking Time: 0 minutes
Servings: 12

Ingredients:

- 3 apples
- ¼ cup orange juice
- 1 ½ lb. watermelon
- ¾ cup blueberries

Method:

1. Use a star-shaped cookie cutter to cut out stars from the apple and watermelon.
2. Soak the apple stars in orange juice.
3. Thread the apple stars, watermelon stars and blueberries into skewers.
4. Refrigerate for 30 minutes before serving.

Nutritional Value:

- Calories 52
- Total Fat 0 g
- Saturated Fat 0 g
- Cholesterol 0 mg
- Sodium 1 mg
- Total Carbohydrate 14 g
- Dietary Fiber 2 g
- Total Sugars 10 g
- Protein 1 g
- Potassium 134 mg

Roasted Mangoes

Preparation Time: 5 minutes
Cooking Time: 10 minutes
Servings: 4

Ingredients:

- 2 mangoes, peeled and sliced into cubes
- 2 tablespoons coconut flakes
- 2 teaspoons crystallized ginger, chopped
- 2 teaspoons orange zest

Method:

1. Preheat your oven to 350 degrees F.
2. Put the mango cubes in custard cups.
3. Top with the ginger and orange zest.
4. Bake in the oven for 10 minutes.

Nutritional Value:

- Calories 89
- Total Fat 2 g
- Saturated Fat 1 g
- Cholesterol 0 mg
- Sodium 14 mg
- Total Carbohydrate 20 g
- Dietary Fiber 2 g
- Total Sugars 17 g
- Protein 1 g
- Potassium 177 mg

Figs with Yogurt

Preparation Time: 8 hours and 5 minutes
Cooking Time: 0 minutes
Servings: 2

Ingredients:

- 8 oz. low fat yogurt
- ½ teaspoon vanilla
- 2 figs, sliced
- 1 tablespoon walnuts, toasted and chopped
- Lemon zest

Method:

1. Refrigerate yogurt in a bowl for 8 hours.
2. After 8 hours, take it out of the refrigerator and stir in yogurt and vanilla.
3. Stir in the figs.
4. Sprinkle walnuts and lemon zest on top before serving.

Nutritional Value:

- Calories 157
- Total Fat 4 g
- Saturated Fat 1 g
- Cholesterol 7 mg
- Sodium 80 mg
- Total Carbohydrate 24 g
- Dietary Fiber 2 g
- Total Sugars 1 g
- Protein 7 g
- Potassium 557mg

Grilled Peaches

Preparation Time: 5 minutes
Cooking Time: 3 minutes
Servings: 6

Ingredients:

- 1 cup balsamic vinegar
- ⅛ teaspoon ground cinnamon
- 1 tablespoon honey
- 3 peaches, pitted and sliced in half
- 2 teaspoons olive oil
- 6 gingersnaps, crushed

Method:

1. Pour the vinegar into a saucepan.
2. Bring it to a boil.
3. Lower heat and simmer for 10 minutes.
4. Remove from the stove.
5. Stir in cinnamon and honey.
6. Coat the peaches with oil.
7. Grill peaches for 2 to 3 minutes.
8. Drizzle each one with syrup.
9. Top with the gingersnaps.

Nutritional Value:

- Calories 135
- Total Fat 3 g
- Saturated Fat 1 g
- Cholesterol 0 mg
- Sodium 42 mg
- Total Carbohydrate 25 g
- Dietary Fiber 2 g
- Total Sugars 18 g
- Protein 1 g
- Potassium 251 mg

Fruit Salad

Preparation Time: 5 minutes
Cooking Time: 0 minute
Servings: 6

Ingredients:

- 8 oz. light cream cheese
- 6 oz. Greek yogurt
- 1 tablespoon honey
- 1 teaspoon orange zest
- 1 teaspoon lemon zest
- 1 orange, sliced into sections
- 3 kiwi fruit, peeled and sliced
- 1 mango, cubed
- 1 cup blueberries

Method:

1. Beat cream cheese using an electric mixer.
2. Add yogurt and honey.
3. Beat until smooth.
4. Stir in the orange and lemon zest.
5. Toss the fruits to mix.
6. Divide in glass jars.
7. Top with the cream cheese mixture.

Nutritional Value:

- Calories 131
- Total Fat 3 g
- Saturated Fat 2 g
- Cholesterol 9 mg
- Sodium 102 mg
- Total Carbohydrate 23 g
- Dietary Fiber 3 g
- Total Sugars 18 g
- Protein 5 g
- Potassium 234 mg

Strawberry & Watermelon Pops

Preparation Time: 6 hours and 10 minutes
Cooking Time: 0 minutes
Servings: 6

Ingredients:

- ¾ cup strawberries, sliced
- 2 cups watermelon, cubed
- ¼ cup lime juice
- 2 tablespoons brown sugar
- ⅛ teaspoon salt

Method:

1. Put the strawberries inside popsicle molds.
2. In a blender, pulse the rest of the ingredients until well mixed.
3. Pour the puree into a sieve before pouring into the molds.
4. Freeze for 6 hours.

Nutritional Value:

- Calories 57
- Total Fat 0 g
- Saturated Fat 0 g
- Cholesterol 0 mg
- Sodium 180 mg
- Total Carbohydrate 14 g
- Dietary Fiber 2 g
- Total Sugars 11 g
- Protein 1 g
- Potassium 180 mg

Conclusion

Just because you have diabetes, it does not mean the end of the world for you.
You can still very much enjoy your life, as well as enjoy delicious dishes.
Hopefully, the recipes in this book will help make sure that you are able to create meals that are both delicious and nutritious.
Have a great life ahead!

Made in the USA
Coppell, TX
26 April 2021